MEDITATIONS

ON THE

ACTUAL STATE OF CHRISTIANITY,

AND ON

THE ATTACKS WHICH ARE NOW BEING MADE UPON IT.

By M. GUIZOT.

TRANSLATED UNDER THE SUPERINTENDENCE OF THE AUTHOR.

NEW YORK:
CHARLES SCRIBNER & CO.,
654 BROADWAY.

PREFACE.

When I published, two years ago, the first series of these *Meditations*, the series which had for its object the essence of Christianity, "that is to say, the natural problems to which Christianity is the answer, the fundamental dogmas by which it solves those problems, and the supernatural facts upon which those dogmas repose," I indicated the general plan of the work which I so commenced, and the order into which its different parts would be distributed.

"Next to the essence of the Christian Religion," I said in my Preface, "comes its history; and this will be the subject of a second series of *Meditations*, in which I shall examine the authenticity of the Scriptures; the primary causes of the foundation of Christianity; Christian faith, as it has always existed throughout its different ages and in spite of all its vicissitudes; the great religious crisis in the sixteenth century, which divided the Church and Europe between Romanism and Protestantism; finally, those antichristian crises which, at different epochs and in different countries, have set in question and imperiled Christianity itself, but which dangers it has ever surmounted. The third series of *Meditations* will be consecrated to the study of the actual state of the Christian religion, its internal and external condition. I shall retrace the regeneration of Christianity which occurred among us at the commencement of the nineteenth century, both in the Church of Rome and in the Protestant Churches; the impulse imparted to it at the same epoch by the Spiritualistic Philosophy that then began again to flourish, and the movement in the contrary direction which showed itself very remarkably soon afterward in the resurrection of Materialism, of Pantheism, of Skepticism, and in works of historical criticism.

I shall attempt to determine the idea, and consequently, in my opinion, the fundamental error of these different systems, the avowed and active enemies of Christianity. Finally, in the fourth series of these *Meditations*, I shall endeavor to discriminate and to characterize the future destiny of the Christian religion, and to indicate by what course it is called upon to conquer completely, and to sway morally, this little corner of the universe, termed by us our earth, in which unfold themselves the designs and power of God, just as, doubtless, they do in an infinity of worlds unknown to us."

Still adhering in its entirety to the plan which I thus proposed, I nevertheless now invert the order. I publish the *Meditations* concerning the actual state of Christianity before those which propose for their object its history. I am struck by two circumstances in the actual state of opinions upon religious questions. On the one side, the sentiments contrary to or favorable to Christianity are defining themselves each day with greater precision. Beliefs become firmer beliefs; opinions hostile to them receive fuller developments. On the other side, vacillating minds are occupying themselves more and more with the struggle to which they are witnesses: minds, earnest at once and sincere, feel the disturbing influence of the doctrines hostile to Christianity; many again are uneasy at these doctrines, many demand a refuge from them, without finding it or daring to seek it in the essential facts and principles of the Christian faith. Between the adversaries of Christianity and its defenders the discussion grows each day in importance and gravity; and with it also grows the perplexity in the minds of the spectators. By setting in full light this actual state of the Christian religion, by comparing the forces at its disposal with those of the systems that it combats, I proceed thither where the emergency is the greatest; I betake myself at once to the very field of battle. I shall afterward resume the history of Christianity from its first establishment down to our own time, and then finally consider the prospect open to it in the future.

I regard with very complicated feelings, with feelings of great perplexity, the actual state of my country; its intellectual and moral state as well as its social and its political state. I have a mind full at once of confidence and of disquietude, of hope and of alarm. Whether for good or for evil, the crisis in which the civilized world is plunged is infinitely more serious than our fathers predicted it would be; more so than even we, who are already experiencing from it the most different consequences, believe it ourselves to be. Sublime truths, excellent principles, are intrinsically blended with ideas essentially false and perverse. A noble work of progress, a hideous work of destruction, are in operation simultaneously in men's opinions and in society. Humanity never so floated between heaven and the abyss. It is especially when I regard the generation now advancing, when I hear what they affirm, when I gather a hint of what they desire and hope for, it is especially then that I feel at once sympathy and anxiety. Sentiments of propriety and of generosity abound in those young hearts; they reject, when once convinced of their justice, neither the ideas which they before did not admit, nor the curb to which by the inspiration of the divine law even human ambition does not refuse to submit; but by a strange and deplorable amalgam, good instincts and evil tendencies exist in them simultaneously; ideas the least reconcilable clash together, and persist in them at the same time. The Truth does not rid them of the error; a light indeed shines upon them, but out of a chaotic darkness which that light has not the power to dissipate.

In the presence of this condition of men's minds, under the impulse of the sentiment which it inspires, I publish this second series of *Meditations*. In touching upon the great questions at present under debate in the philosophical world, in expressing my opinion concerning Rationalism, Positivism, Pantheism, Materialism, Skepticism, I have not for a moment pretended to discuss these different systems completely and scientifically. Although I am convinced that they are no more in a condition to support any profound examination of severe reason than to stand the first regard of common sense, the object which I propose to myself is to indicate only their radical and incurable vice. This is no treatise of Metaphysics; it is only an appeal addressed to upright and independent minds; an appeal made to induce them to subject science to the test of the human conscience, and to regard with distrust systems, which, in the name of a pretended scientific truth, would, between the intellectual order and the moral order, between the thought and the life of man, destroy the harmony established by the law of God.

GUIZOT.

VAL-RICHER, *April*, 1866.

CONTENTS.

MEDITATIONS

ON THE ACTUAL STATE OF

THE CHRISTIAN RELIGION.

FIRST MEDITATION.

THE AWAKENING OF CHRISTIANITY IN FRANCE IN THE NINETEENTH CENTURY.

In 1797, La Réveillière-Lépeaux, one of the five Directors who then constituted the government of France, having just read to that class of the Institut* of which he was a member a memorial respecting Theophilanthropism, and the forms suitable for this new worship, consulted Talleyrand upon the subject; the latter replied, "I have but a single observation to

* The class of moral and political sciences.

make: Jesus Christ, to found his religion, suffered himself to be crucified, and he rose again. You should try to do as much."

Nor was it long before events justified the ironical counsel. In 1802, hardly four years afterward, Theophilanthropism and its apostle, the dream and the dreamer, had disappeared from the stage where they had been powerless in influence, barren in consequence. The strong hand of Napoleon again solemnly set up in France the religion of Christ crucified and Christ risen, and in that same year the brilliant genius of Chateaubriand again placed before the eyes of his countrymen the beauties of Christianity. The great politician and the great writer bowed each of them before the Cross; the Cross was the point from which each started —the one to reconstruct the Christian Church in France, the other to prove how capable a Christian writer is of charming French society and of stirring its emotions.

In these days, and in some parts of Christendom, the Concordat and the "Génie du Christianisme," the one as a political institution, the other as a literary production, have lost something of their vogue. Catholics, zealous and sincere, criticise severely the defects of the Concordat; they regard it as sometimes incomplete, sometimes tyrannical: they reproach it with assailing the rights of religious society, of paralyzing its influence, and restricting its liberty. Some go so far as to express wishes for the separation of Church and State, and for their entire independence of each other, the only certain guarantee to either, they affirm, of a real moral influence. Protestants, equally zealous and sincere, entertain the same opinions and the same wishes. Not contented with this, the latter have gone further, and acted; they have separated themselves from the Protestant Church recognized by the State, and have founded independent Churches, self-governing and self-sufficing; nor have they demanded anything from the State but the liberty that is every citizen's due. In a work recently published,* a pastor of one of these Churches, a man distinguished both by the elevation of his mind and the generosity of his sentiments, M. Edmond de Pressensé, has gone still further. Not content with defending the principle of the separation of Church and State, he has endeavored to prove that, in 1802, the Concordat was, on the part of Napoleon, simply an act of tyranny and ambition; that it was, as far as Christianity is concerned, an untoward incident; and that if the Christian Church, at the time spontaneously regenerating itself, had been left free and uncontrolled, it would have risen by its own proper strength, and would have grown in influence and in faith far more than the Concordat has permitted it to do. I am far from proposing to discuss here, as a general proposition, the system of separation of Church and State, or its worth in a religious or social point of view;

* L'Église et la Révolution française, histoire des relations de l'Église et de l'État, de 1789–1802. 8vo. 1864.

such a system I do not regard as the ideal of religious society: the co-existence, I would rather say the competition, of Churches recognized by the State and of Dissenting Churches independently constituting themselves and self-sufficing, is, in my opinion, the system most in conformity with the nature of things, and most favorable to the solidity and general efficiency of religion. That is a question rather of epoch, time, manners, and social condition than of principle. But, however this may be, I hold it as certain that, in 1802, the Concordat was, on the part of Napoleon, far more an act of superior sagacity than of arbitrary power, and that it was for the Christian religion in France an event as salutary as necessary. After the anarchy and the orgies of the Revolution, nothing but the solemn recognition of Christianity by the State could have given satisfaction to the public sentiment, and insured to the religion of Christ the dignity and the stability, the recovery of which was so essential to its influence. Nothing is more liable to error than an attempt to appreciate, with reference to present circumstances and the actual condition of men's minds, what was possible and good sixty years ago; and I am convinced, that in spite of his zeal for the separation of Church and State, M. Edmond de Pressensé, had he lived in 1802, would have been as little satisfied as France herself with a Christian Church restored in accordance with the plan of the Abbé Grégoire. The Concordat was a mixed and imperfect measure, subject to grave objections, and the source of numberless difficulties; but, taken altogether, the measure was grand and salutary; it gave at once to the Christian movement a sanction and an impulse that no other scheme would have been capable of imparting.

M. de Chateaubriand and the "Génie du Christianisme" are entitled to the same justice. I am ready, with regard to both book and author, to concede the truth of all the objections and of all the defects that the severest critic may be able or may wish to detect; their grand and salutary action will not be the less a living fact. It is with books as it is with men; it is by their qualities, whatever their faults, that they command position and exercise sway, and wherever superior qualities are discernible, their efficacy remains in spite of any faults, in spite of any defects, by which they may be accompanied. Notwithstanding its imperfections in a religious and literary point of view, the "Génie du Christianisme" was in both these respects a performance at the same time remarkable and powerful: it strongly moved men's minds, it gave a fresh impulse to men's imaginations, it reanimated and placed in their proper rank the traditions and the early impressions of Christianity. No criticism, however legitimate, can ever deprive that work of the place that it at once assumed in the religious and the literary history of its time and country.

Neither the Concordat nor the "Génie du Christianisme" was, in 1802, the result of a spirit of blind and barren reaction. Napoleon and Chateaubriand were both of them hardy innovators. At the side of the ancient religion which he re-established, Napoleon firmly maintained also the liberty of conscience, whether in matters of worship or philosophy. At the very instant when the Concordat was proclaimed and the "Génie du Christianisme" was published, the learned physiologist, Cabanis, also published his treatise on the relations of man's physical and moral nature, a work which characterized man as a mere machine. And in recalling France to an admiration of the beauties of Christian literature, Chateaubriand imaged them to her in forms of language so novel and so original, that many among the severe guardians of the French language treated him as an outrageous and barbarous writer. A new era opened at this epoch in France for religion and for literature. Christianity and systems opposed to Christianity, Roman Catholicism, Protestantism, and Philosophy, a taste for classics, and a tendency to romanticism, unfolded themselves simultaneously, surprised to be living together, and at the same time encountering one another as ardent combatants.

I have no design to retrace here their contests nor to constitute myself their judge. Let but a great arena be thrown open, and the crowd rushes in, carrying with it its confusion and its buzz. Happily, the tumult is not of long duration. In this mighty movement of men's minds in France at the commencement of the nineteenth century I occupy myself with a single grand fact—the Awakening of Christianity, its different characteristics, its different results. The crisis itself had illustrious witnesses. I will interrogate these alone.

After Napoleon and Chateaubriand, the first whom I meet with are two Catholic writers, who have left behind them great and deserved reputations. M. de Bonald and M. de Maistre hoisted the banner of Christianity valiantly, and at an early date. But their ideas and their writings were rather political than religious: the exigencies of public order occupied their attention far more than those of man's soul, and their works were rather attacks upon the French Revolution than a defense of the faith of Christians. By a coincidence very remarkable, although at the same time very natural, the first production of each — "The Theory of Power," by M. de Bonald, and the "Considerations on France," by M. de Maistre—was published at the same moment, in 1796, and each in a foreign land, where the authors were living as emigrants. In the first ardor of the reaction, and with the impassioned and vague feelings that it suggested, each wrote against the Revolution that shook the world and wrecked his own fortunes. Potent intelligences both, profound moralists, eminent writers; but their philosophy is a philosophy of circumstance and of party. Their theories they use as arms; their books as a discharge. M. de Bonald is a lofty-minded original thinker, but subtle, too, and complex; disposed to content himself with verbal combinations and distinctions, and sparing no labor to contrive his vast web of arguments proper to entrap the unwary adversary. M. de Maistre, on the contrary, blasts him with the absoluteness of his assertion, the poignancy of his irony, the rude eloquence of his invectives. He is a powerful, a charming extemporizer. Both of them excel in seizing and presenting in a striking manner one great side, but only one of the great sides, in questions or measures. They see not these in their variety and in their entirety. Combatants approved—the one tenacious, the other impetuous—they both committed two grave faults: they instituted a closer bond between statesmanship and religion than is proper or suitable to either; they could not discover any other remedy for anarchy than absolutism. In the natural and never-ending conflict of the two great forces whose co-existence imparts vital energy to human society—authority and liberty—they declared for the former alone, thus ignoring the right of thought, the spirit of our times, and the general course of Christian civilization. When attacked in her essence, Religion should be defended as she was founded, in herself and for herself, setting aside every political consideration, and in the name alone of the problems which lay siege to man's soul, and of the relations of man's soul with God. "Render unto Cesar the things which are Cesar's, and unto God the things that are God's," said Jesus to the Pharisees when they sought to embarrass and to compromise him politically. Thus did Jesus himself define the proper and paramount characteristic of his work. He did not come to destroy or to found any government; he came to feed, to regulate, and to save the human soul, leaving to time and to the natural efficacy of events the development of the social consequence of his religious faith and of his religious law. M. de Bonald and M. de Maistre joined too often together God and Cesar. They thought too much of Cesar while defending God. In doing this they changed and compromised the character of that great movement, the Awakening of Christianity, which their conduct otherwise provoked and served.*

After these two great writers, another great

* "The dead move quick," says the poet Bürger in his ballad of Leonora. The men and the books I record died at a period already distant from us; and in spite of their fame that abides, they are probably little known to the generation at present in possession of the stage. I regard it, therefore, as not improper for me to mention below the titles of their principal works, of which I have in the text sought to determine the true character.

Those of M. de Bonald are:

1. La Théorie du pouvoir politique et religieux. 3 vols. 8vo. Constance: 1796.

2. La Législation primitive. 3 vols. 8vo. Paris: 1821.

3. L'Essai sur le divorce. 1 vol. 8vo. Paris.

4. Les Recherches philosophique. 2 vols. 8vo. 1818 and 1826.

5. Les Mélanges littéraires et politiques. 2 vols. 8vo.

6. Pensées et discours. 2 vols. 8vo.

All these writings, with some others, have been collected in the complete edition of the works of M. de Bonald, in seven volumes. 8vo. Paris: 1854.

The principal works of M. de Maistre are:

1. Considérations sur la France. 1 vol. 8vo. 1796.

2. Essai sur le principe générateur des constitutions politiques et des autres institutions humaines. 1 vol. 8vo. 1810.

3. Du Pape. 2 vols. 8vo. 1819.

writer, (shall I term him Catholic?) the Abbé de la Mennais, placed himself upon the same path, but to arrive at a very different issue. He, too, made authority alone the basis of man's faith and of human society; but seeking to ascertain the sign which distinguishes legitimate authority, and which entitles it to unarguing submission, he fixed this sign in the general and traditional assent of mankind. "The common consent or authority, *there*," said he, "we find the natural rule of our judgment; and what but folly can reject that rule, and listen to its own reason in preference to the reason of all? . . . The search for certitude is the search for a reason not liable to error at all, that is, for a reason that is infallible. Now this infallible reason must necessarily be either the reason of

4. De l'Église gallicane dans son rapport avec le souverain pontife. 8vo. 1821.

5. Examen de la philosophie de Bacon. 2 vols. 8vo. 1836.

6. Soirées de Saint-Pétersbourg. 2 vols. 8vo.

7. Lettres et opuscules inédits. 2 vols. 8vo. 1851.

8. Mémoires politiques et correspondance du comte de Maistre, publiés par M. Albert Blanc. 2 vols. 8vo. 1858.

each individual or the reason of all men; in fact, of human reason. It is not the reason of each individual, for men contradict one another, and nothing frequently is more discordant and more contradictory than their judgments; therefore it is the reason of all." *

In holding this language in his very first work, the Abbé de la Mennais was already forgetting that he was a Christian and a Catholic. When a man demands here below an infallible authority, he must not seek it from any human source. The reason of all? (That is, the reason of the majority of men in all the ages of the world, for the reason of *all* is a fallacy.) What is such reason, but the sovereignty of superior numbers in the spiritual order? Having fixed his principle, the Abbé de la Mennais kept it in sight everywhere. After having established an infallible authority in the name of the reason of all, he proclaimed the absolute

* Essai sur l'indifférence en matière de religion, t. ii, p. 59. Défense de l'Essai sur l'indifférence, chap. x, pp. 133–148.

sovereignty in the name of universal suffrage. But this apostle of universal reason was at the same time the proudest worshiper of his own reason. Under the pressure of events without, and of an ardent controversy, a transformation took place in him, marked at once by its logical deductions and its moral inconsistency: he changed his camp without changing his principles; in the attempt to lead the supreme authority of his Church to admit his principles he had failed; and from that instant the very spirit of revolt that he had so severely rebuked broke loose in his soul and in his writings, finding expression at one time in an indignation full of hatred leveled at the powerful, the rich, and the fortunate ones of the world; at another time in a tender sympathy for the miseries of humanity. The "Words of a Believer" are the eloquent outburst of this tumult in his soul. Plunged in the chaos of sentiments the most contradictory, and yet claiming to be always consistent with himself, the champion of authority became in the State the most baited of democrats, and in the Church the haughtiest of rebels.

It is not without sorrow that I thus express my unreserved opinion of a man of superior talent—mind lofty, soul intense; a man in the sequel profoundly sad himself, although haughty in his very fall. One cannot read in their stormy succession the numerous writings of the Abbé de la Mennais without recognizing in them traces, I will not say of his intellectual perplexities—his pride did not feel them—but of the sufferings of his soul, whether for good or for evil. A noble nature, but full of exaggeration in his opinions, of fanatical arrogance, and of angry asperity in his polemics. One title to our gratitude remains to the Abbé de la Mennais—he thundered to purpose against the gross and vulgar forgetfulness of the great moral interests of humanity. His essay on indifference in religious questions inflicted a rude blow upon that vice of the time, and recalled men's souls to regions above. And thus it was that he, too, rendered service to the great movement and awakening of Christians in the nineteenth century, and that he merits his place in that movement although he deserted it.*

At the same time that great minds were thus at work in order to restore to the belief in Christianity and the belief in Catholicism its honor and its authority, another influence was operating in the same direction, with less notoriety but no less effect. The Jesuits were re-establishing themselves

* The principal works of the Abbé de la Mennais are:

1. L'Essai sur l'indifférence en matière de religion, avec la défense de l'Essai. 5 vols. 8vo. The first volume appeared in 1817.

2. De la Religion considérée dans ses rapports avec l'ordre civil et politique. 1 vol. 8vo. 1825.

3. Les Paroles d'un Croyant. 8vo. 1834.

4. Les Affaires de Rome. 8vo. 1836.

5. Esquisse d'une philosophie. 4 vols. 8vo. 1841–1846.

All his works, including numerous pamphlets and articles published in religious and political journals, have been collected in two editions: one in 12 vols. 8vo., 1836–1837; the other in 11 vols. 8vo., 1844 and following years. Besides the above, there are his Posthumous Works, 2 vols. 8vo., 1856, and his Correspondence, 2 vols. 8vo., 1858.

in France—were founding houses of education and noviciates for their order—were opening chapels, preaching, teaching, careless of the existence in France of laws proscribing them; occupying themselves solely with fulfilling what they regarded as a duty, and a duty, too, springing from a right believed by them to be superior to the laws. That duty for them was to uphold the Church of Rome; that right was the right of preaching and teaching, according to the faith of the Church. The Jesuits have also been considered and represented as politicians in the garb of monks, rather than genuine members of the monastic orders. Often, in effect, in their acts and in their words, they have appeared as politicians, and politicians, too, with a certain indulgence for the world and the world's masters; but, at bottom, they have been and they are essentially monastic—an order perhaps the most ardent of all, for they are of all orders the order most completely devoted to the cause of religious authority.

There are commonplaces that have to be continually repeated, so apt are men to forget them. In religious society, as well as in civil society, there are two great moral forces—Authority and Liberty; these coexist of necessity—have dominion turn by turn, and have alternately their heroes and their martyrs. Regarded either with respect to its political or religious constitution, society cannot long dispense with either Authority or with Liberty; and each of these two forces is liable to abuse its influence, and to lose it by the very abuse.

When Authority has had a long dominion, and its abuse too has been long, a reaction occurs: Liberty has her revenge; but in her turn is prone to compromise her interests by abuses and by excess. It is the history of all human society; facts prove it quite as much as common sense foretells it. In the bosom of this general fact it is the peculiar character, as it is the glory, of Christianity that it has fully accepted these two rival forces; and the one in the face of the other—authority and liberty—both of divine origin. Christianity has constantly accounted them for such as they are—the one the revealed law of God, the other the innate right of man, whom God created free and responsible. The history of the Jews is only that of the intimate and continued relations between God as sovereign and man as free agent; God uttering and giving the law, man using his liberty at one time to fulfill, at another to reject, the law of God. When the great day of humanity dawned and Jesus came, it was in liberty's name, and in claiming the right of the soul to obey the divine law according to its convictions, that Christianity engaged in its primitive struggle of three centuries. Under this banner, too, it conquered, and under it religious society and civil society combined without becoming identical. The tempestuous and painful fecundity of the middle ages succeeded to the tyrannical unity of the Roman empire, so sterile in result. Hence principles the most inconsistent, issues the most contradictory—the power of religion and the power of the state—popes and kings now supporting, now combating each other's ambitious purposes, and thwarting each other's measures, without any regard to law or right; liberty sometimes suffering cruelly by their alliance, sometimes happily profiting by their dissensions; on some occasions popes, on others monarchs protecting liberty against their reciprocal pretensions and excesses. Spiritual and temporal princes still wavered in their maxims and in their policy, and did not during the middle ages systematically and on all occasions form coalitions, of which liberty was to pay the cost. Liberty, on the contrary, continued to subsist and to grow in the midst of their rivalries and of her own sufferings. But these rivalries and these sufferings produced a chaos which recurred incessantly, and became ever more and more intolerable, precisely on account of the progress still made, and which no effort could stifle. The great body of Christians at last demanded some issue from this chaos; then those who wielded the religious power and the civil power, now separately, now in concert, endeavored to satisfy the craving of the world; and by their councils, pragmatic sanctions, encyclical letters and concordats, sought to reform the abuses and the grievances which, as men loudly proclaimed, existed, if not in the Church itself, at least in the relations of the Church with the State. Whether from want of wisdom, virtue, courage, or sagacity in their authors, or from their measures being too superficial, or meeting with too much opposition, those attempts failed; and the reform that was to have proceeded from Authority herself remained without accomplishment. Then came the reform by insurrection, in the name of Faith and Liberty; and as happens in similar crises, whether of the Church or the State, the supreme authority of Romanism was attacked, not only in its abuses and its vices, but in its principle and its very existence.

Rome then committed the fault almost always committed by Power when seriously menaced—it defended itself by pushing its principle and its right to the extreme, without holding account of any other principle or of any other right. In the name of Unity and Infallibility in matters of faith, the supreme power in the Church of Rome allied itself with the absolute power in the State, and supported the latter in its resistance to liberty. Under the inspiration of their founder and hero, Loyola, whose genius was that of a fanatic and a mystic, but who was adroit in organizing and realizing his design, the order of the Jesuits sprung into existence. This order was born of this war and for this war—a chosen troop, charged in the name of the faith to be the uncompromising defenders of authority in Church and in State.

Since that epoch three centuries have passed, and the fourth is in its turn sweeping by us; neither times nor chances have been wanting to causes to produce their effects, nor to men to accomplish their designs; principles and events have received their development over a vast space; and in the light of heaven the different systems have been put to the test of successes and of reverses. Absolutism has had its triumphs and its victories; more than once the faults of its adversaries have played into its hands, and it has found able and glorious champions. It has not succeeded in arresting the course of a civilization full of liberty and yet still greedy to have more. It has taken its place in the midst of liberty as a temporary necessity, never as a preponderating tendency. More than this, even in the epochs when its influence was its height, and its splendor the greatest, Absolutism has often served the cause hostile to its own. Louis XIV. seconded the movement of mind and the people's progress; Napoleon sowed in every direction the germs of social advancement or innovation. And now, even there, where liberty does not exist, Absolutism does not avow itself; it furls its banner, and admits institutions contrary to its principles, reserving to itself the right to elude, or to render them powerless. Experience has pronounced its judgment; whatever the problems that the future will have to solve, or the trials which the future will have to encounter, the cause of Absolutism is a lost cause throughout Christendom.

At the commencement of this century, the Jesuits, unfortunately for them, and yet very naturally, were regarded as devoted to that cause. After having served it in the eighteenth century, they had been the first victims of its decline; the papal and the monarchical sovereignty had sacrificed them to the new opinions, just as mariners in a tempest throw overboard their heavy ordnance. When the nineteenth century opened, all was greatly changed; the Revolution was not only victorious, but earnestly engaged in conciliating parties by disavowing and making amends for its excesses. After the commission of so many follies and crimes in the pursuit of liberty, France submitted once more with the greatest satisfaction to the voice of authority.

How would they then reconstruct that French policy that had been at once so overthrown and so regenerated? By what means would they conciliate new and ancient ideas, new and ancient interests? Upon what terms would Authority and Liberty consent to be reconciled, and to live henceforth side by side—Authority soaring triumphant after her fall, Liberty embarrassed with her recent excesses; and yet both of them more than ever necessary to society, if society was to be healthy and strong? This was evidently the vital question of the new century. God placed its solution at first in the hands of Napoleon, the crown and the scourge of the Revolution, the most remarkable example at once of reaction and of progress recorded in the history of the world.

In this condition, so new to France, the situation of the Jesuits was embarrassing and perilous. Napoleon was again re-establishing the Church of Rome, and at the same time enforcing the maxims of Absolutism—a double title to their sympathy. On the other hand, he was consolidating the Revolution, and maintaining and putting into practice some of its essential principles, among others, that of freedom of conscience. Napoleon arrogated also to himself the right of dictating and acting as master in the Church as in the State, at Rome as at Paris; he was neither a serious believer in the faith of Christ nor a sure friend of the Papacy. In this twofold aspect, the Jesuits could not but regard him with distrust. The distrust was mutual: for if Napoleon was for the Jesuits a too faithful and too ambitous heir of the Revolution, the Jesuits were for him Catholics too independent and too devoted to their Church and to its chief. As far back as 1804, their establishments, scarcely disguised under different names, had been a source of disquietude to Napoleon. He directed them to be closed, enforced the laws which denied to religious corporations an independent existence, and founded the University, which at the same time he invested with the privilege of teaching.

This system was not abolished at the Restoration. The Jesuits then entered into the simultaneous possession of two forces novel to them —the one sprang from the support of power, the other was derived from the progress of liberty. They had the favor of the court, and might wield as their own arms, and in their own interests, the liberal principles that were dear to the people. A position excellent, had they known how to restrict themselves to their religious mission, keep aloof from political contests, and devote themselves exclusively to the task of awakening the faith of Christians, and arousing them to a Christian life! Their action upon the soul might have extended their influence beyond their peculiar sphere to the world without. Had they not then a striking instance of such an influence even in their own order? To what cause, thirty years ago, did the Père Ravignan owe the respect and moral authority with which he was surrounded, not only by members of his own Church, but by men not remarkable for their faith? Far less to his talent as an orator, than to the thorough sincerity and disinterestedness of his religious character. He was a believer, a pious Christian, and a stranger to every mental reservation; neither was he a partisan, but solely occupied with the service of God, of his Church, and of his order, at the same time that he was propagating the faith and enforcing piety. He declared himself aloud a Jesuit, but the declaration excited no distrust even in his adversaries. If his order had imitated his example, it would have obtained a similar success. Nor was the instance new. In the seventeenth century, at the court of Louis XIV., Bourdaloue displayed the same virtues as the Père Ravignan in our own days; and, in all certitude, did more honor and rendered more service to his Church and order than had ever been done or rendered by Père la Chaise.

I shall not attempt to examine how far the Jesuits in effect were really engaged, or what was the degree of their direct agency in the intrigues of the retrograde party who were seeking to repossess themselves of the relics of the ancient institutions, in the idle hope of reconstructing the social edifice upon those ruined foundations. I am convinced that France felt at this epoch far too much alarm for this party and its allies, Jesuits or no Jesuits, just as the Monarchy itself felt too much apprehension of the Revolutionists. No graver fault can be committed by nations or by governments than to give way to fears out of proportion with the dangers which they encounter. France had no reason under the Restoration to dread either the triumph of Theocracy or of Absolutism; and yet she was alarmed at both, and the people persisted in believing that the Jesuits were serving this double cause—that of the ancient régime of the Papacy, and of the ancient régime of the Monarchy. The Jesuits had then to struggle at once against the ideas and the passions of modern society, and the traditions and maxims of ancient France herself; they had for adversaries, the laity, the bar, and the liberals, respectively represented by M. de Montlosier, M. Benjamin Constant, and M. Dupin. The odds against them were too great; even the Monarchy itself, however well disposed toward them, was carried away by the movement which attacked them, and Charles X. did not think his own position strong enough to dispense with treating them, by his ordonnances of the 21st June, 1828, as Napoleon had done by his decree of the 22d June, 1804. Throughout this whole period the conduct of the Jesuits was feebler than their cause. Sworn and devoted to the defense of Authority, they had not foresight enough to perceive by what means and on what conditions Authority might raise and consolidate itself. Haunted by the traditions of past times, and having the history of their own order continually before their minds, they no longer regarded the future boldly or confidently; they failed to appreciate justly the present; they did not believe sufficiently in the power of Christ's faith, and they believed too implicitly in the efficiency of worldly policy. By this vulgar blunder they compromised, in the case of many Christians, the full effect of that great stirring movement of Christianity, at the very time that, with respect to others, they aided it materially.

The Revolution of 1830 inflicted a rude blow upon these retrograde tendencies, and a new element started up in the bosom of the Church of Rome. In the midst of the grand manifestation and progress of liberty now realizing itself in the State, Catholics, genuine and ardent too, conceived the hope of turning both to the profit of the Church of Rome, and of at last setting Catholicism at peace and in harmony with the new social institutions of France. Then the group, I will not say the party, formed itself of men at once generous and hardy, who did not hesitate to declare themselves Ultramontanists, like the Père de Ravignan, Liberals like M. de la Fayette. It consisted of priests and laymen, of men of mature years and men in the spring-time of life —the Abbé Lacordaire, Abbe Gerbet, M. de Montalembert, and M. de Coux: I confine myself to the names that at the outset gleamed on their banners. They founded an *agency* for the defense of the liberties of religion, and a journal, the *Avenir*, to develop its principles and its constitution. But the association was born under an unlucky star; for its little army had for its declared chief, and the object of its passionate reverence, the Abbe de la Mennais. In the more intimate and unrestricted relations of life this great man appears to have exercised extraordinarily attractive power over his friends and disciples. Cited jointly with him on the 31st January, 1831, before the Cour d'Assises of Paris to answer for the appearance of two articles in the *Avenir*, the Abbé Lacordaire said, "I stand here near the man who began the reconciliation of Catholicism with the world. Let me tell him how affected I am by the part that God has made for me in giving me him as my master and my father. Suffer these words of filial piety to penetrate to the heart of one so long misunderstood; suffer me to exclaim with the poet:

"L'amitié d'un grand homme est un bienfait des dieux."*

The Abbé Lacordaire had soon to feel the danger and to repel with sorrow the yoke of this seductive friendship. The errors and the evil passions of the Abbé de la Mennais were not long in exploding; his was a mind lofty and powerful, but without grasp, without foresight, without moderation, and without equity; incapable of discerning the different sides of a subject and of embracing all the

* "A great man's friendship, blessed gift of Heaven."

elements of the problem demanding solution, he was a haughty slave to the truth that he served but partially, and the somber enemy of every one who wounded his pride by contesting his opinions. He gave to the *Avenir* a character at once democratic and theocratic, imperious and revolutionary. All the ideas contrary to his own, all the institutions, all the governments, that stood in his way, were attacked by him with a degree of vehemence, insult, and menace never surpassed by any political partisan, however violent. The maxims of the Gallican Church were, to cite his words, "an object of disgust and horror; opinions as odious as they were base, which, while rendering even the conscience the accomplice of tyranny, make servility a duty and brute force an independent and just right." He demanded the separation of Church and State as a necessity absolute and urgent; "for," said he, "we regard as abolished and of no effect every particular law which contradicts the Charter, and is incompatible with the liberties that *it* proclaims. In the event of such law, we believe that it becomes immediately and without delay the duty of government to come to an understanding with the pope, and to rescind the Concordat, which lost all the means of being executed from the instant when, thank God, the Catholic religion ceased to be a state religion." Four months had scarcely elapsed since the birth of the government of July, and because the liberty of teaching promised by the Charter of 1830 was not already in vigor, the Abbé de la Mennais said to the Catholics: "Whence comes the oppression that weighs upon us? Either, in what concerns us, the government cannot or it will not keep its promises. If it cannot, what is this mockery of a sovereignty, this miserable phantom of government, and what have we to do with it? It is as far as we are concerned as if it were *not*, and nothing remains to us but to forget it, and seek our safety in ourselves. Let us proclaim aloud who the powers are that are hostile to us; whose servants seek only to satisfy blindly their thirst for persecution." What attacks leveled at a government were ever more precipitate, more violent, and showed a less just appreciation of facts? What revolutionary party ever proclaimed with greater audacity disobedience to the laws, and insurrection as the first of rights and of duties?

Side by side with these violent and insulting invectives leveled at the government of France, the *Avenir* placed a declaration of respect and submission to the chief of the Church of Rome: "We profess," it said, "the most complete obedience to the authority of the Vicar of Jesus Christ. We will not have other faith than his faith, other doctrine than his doctrine. All that he approves we approve, all that he condemns we condemn, and without the shadow of a reservation; we, each of us, submit to the judgment of the Holy See all our past, all our future writings, of what nature soever they may be." Here, at least, the revolutionary spirit seemed absent, or, at all events, was in a hurry to disavow itself.

I am persuaded that, in holding this language, the Abbé de la Mennais was sincere. When an exclusive idea or passion sways a man's mind, nothing is more unknown to him than his own future conduct; he knows even less what he will do than what he is doing. The Abbé de la Mennais no more suspected in 1831 what he would say and what he would do a few years later, than the most violent leaders of the French Revolution suspected in 1789 what they would be and what they would do in 1793. The court at Rome was clearer-sighted than its fanatical champion; it had been under the influence of the charm of the first works and of the first successes of the Abbé de la Mennais. It had not, however, failed to perceive what pernicious and dangerous seed might thence germinate. The *Avenir* occasioned it profound disquietude; the principles and the yearnings of modern society found therein a too ready acceptance; the régime which had governed France since 1830 was too much the object of its attacks; it demanded too much liberty, and made too much noise in doing so; for beneath that noise, and in the shadow of that liberty, fermented the anarchical doctrines and tendencies which in all cases and places it is the aim and the policy of the court of Rome to contest. Thus the *Avenir* and its writers placed her in a position full of embarrassment; Rome was anxious neither in any way to ignore the services that they had rendered and that they might continue to render her, nor to lose sight of the perils that they made her incur; Rome desired to preserve silence respecting these writers—neither to avow nor disavow them—and to leave it to time to terminate their transport and their errors. The Abbé de la Mennais did not, however, permit this expectant policy; he insisted absolutely that the papacy, by pronouncing upon his doctrines and upon his attitude, should publicly either give him her support or withdraw it from him. All the world knows of the journey which he undertook in 1831 to Rome to obtain this result, and of his stay there in company with the Abbé Lacordaire and M. de Montalembert, "three obscure Christians"—to use the words of the Abbé de la Mennais—men who thought themselves called, according to the expression of the Abbé Lacordaire before the Cour d'Assises at Paris, "to reconcile Catholicism with the world." The Pope (Gregory XVI.) judged otherwise, and by his encyclical of the 15th August, 1832, with regret, but at the same time with as much decision as to the substantial matters before him as tenderness to the three pilgrims personally, condemned the *Avenir*, its doctrines, and its tendencies. On the instant, with the concurrence of their friends, they declared, all three, (10th September, 1832,) that, respectfully submitting themselves to the authority of the Vicar of Jesus Christ, they abandoned the lists in which they had faithfully combated during the past two years; that, in consequence, the *Avenir*, which had been provisionally suspended ever since the 15th November previously, would no longer appear, and that the *General Agency for the Defense of Religious Liberty* was dissolved.

As the first declaration of the writers of the *Avenir*, after their acquittal by the Cour d'Assises at Paris, had been sincere, so was also the declaration sincere which was published by them immediately after their condemnation by the papacy; but they promised more than they could perform. When a deep social wound has been laid bare, and measures on a large scale have been adopted to cure it, it is no longer in the power of any individual to keep that wound secret, or to stifle the hope of a remedy. How many times in the course of this century has not the papacy, and have not the ardent champions of liberty, condemned and combated the efforts made to reconcile Catholicism with modern civilization, and to cause the Church to accept the liberties of civil society, and the State to recognize the rights of the Church? How often has the Church by its censures signalized such efforts as impious and suicidal? What wit, what eloquence, have not been displayed by the Liberals to declare their vanity, their worthlessness? To what reproaches, invectives, and sarcasms have not their advocates had to submit? But no ecclesiastical censure, no wrath of religion, no mockery of liberalism has arrested the march of this great idea. It has made, and it continues every day to force, its way in spite of condemnations, attacks, and obstacles of every description. Why? For paramount reasons, impossible to be lost sight of. For Christianity and modern civilization confront each other; there exists in the public a profound and irrepressible feeling of their reciprocal right and strength—a profound and irrepressible feeling that their disagreement is an immense evil for society and for men's souls; that neither the new civil liberties nor the ancient forms of belief and influences of Christianity can ever perish; that, necessary, both of them, to nations and to individuals, they are both of them destined to live, and consequently to live together. When and in what manner will this feeling realize its object, and when will the ancient Church and modern civilization have solved the problem of their mutual pacification? No one can at this moment pronounce; but in all certitude, the problem will not for that cease to weigh upon the world, or the world to strive at its solution. Even the men who, in a spirit of pious submission or in a paroxysm of sadness and discouragement might wish, after having attempted it, to renounce the work, could never remain inactive before a necessity becoming more and more urgent; they doubtless would not be long before they returned to the lists from which they might have consented to withdraw.

And this is what happened to the three eminent men who had made so precipitate a journey to Rome, and had importuned her at an inconvenient moment, summoning her at once to solve the momentous questions they had raised. They returned from Rome with the intention of submitting to the decision of the Pope; but slumber to such souls was impossible, and it was not long before men saw them, the three, resuming, although by the most contrary paths, all the activity of their minds and of their lives. The Abbé de la Mennais threw himself with impetuosity into the revolt—a revolt radical against the Church and against the State; furiously demanding from the populace and from revolutions the success which he could not obtain in the bosom of order, and in concert with the authority previously so ardently defended by him. Far from following in his new and violent course, the Abbé Lacordaire and M. de Montalembert separated from him, and returned each to his natural and tranquil position; the one to that of a simple priest, almoner of the convent of the Visitation, and preacher in the chapel of the College Stanislas; the other to that of a young and brilliant political orator, already a favorite in the chamber of Peers, although its members did not always think or vote with him. Both remained Romanists at heart; they zealously shared in the great movement of Christianity, now roused from her slumber, but without ceasing to be Liberals in their Catholicism, or without arresting their efforts to reconcile the Church with the régime of liberty.

The position of each, and the genius of each, determined the share that he took in the duties, and the place that he selected for the field of his action. The Abbé Lacordaire, from the pulpit of Notre Dame, developed, or rather let me say, painted, in all their splendor, the truths, the beauties, the moral and social excellences of the Christian Faith and of the Catholic Church. M. de Montalembert, in the house of Peers and in literature, was the ardent and indefatigable champion of the Church, of its maxims, and of its rights. To neither was there any lack of success any more than any lack of talent and of zeal. A numerous auditory, young and old, from the salons and from the schools, believers and freethinkers, flocked round the Abbé Lacordaire, all feeling the attraction, and almost all the charm; many among them yielding to the persuasion of that eloquence so fresh and vivid, and abundant, and unlooked for—impetuous without rudeness, hardy yet graceful, natural even where there was temerity of thought or of expression, and repairing or vailing these faults by the enchantment of candor and of originality. Different, but not inferior, were the merits and the successes of M. de Montalembert. He was a combatant young too, a fearless Christian, both in the political arena and in society; and he carried with him in his polemics to the service of the State a sincerity of passion, a rich and mobile eloquence, piquant strokes of wit, an outpouring of indignant conviction, all of which deeply stirred the emotions of his auditors, whether friends or adversaries, and left in the mind of calm spectators an impression of approving satisfaction, however frequently a shock might be given to their feelings of moderation and of fairness. In the "Conferences" of the Abbé Lacordaire it cannot be denied that many failings and many omissions are observable; although expressed clearly and with vivacity, his thought was often superficial; there was in turn a singular mixture of precipitate enthusiasm and of discretion, the former displaying itself in his exordiums, the latter at the close of his discourses. He announced courageously his opinions, but accompanied them by more reservations than are usually expected from one of his Church and party: thus at the same time, that throughout all his discourses, and in their general character, he showed himself the friend of religious liberty, he hesitated sometimes even when the occasion required him to proclaim its fundamental principle and to rebuke its violations. On his side,

M. de Montalembert gave himself up entirely to the impression and the combat of the moment; in his legitimate ardor for free instruction, the then chosen object of his public life, he held obstacles, however real, of no account; he ignored the time necessary for its final triumph, as well as the real progress, although partial, which it had obtained, from the co-operation or the sufferance of the government of 1830; and in his uncompromising defense of the Church, he was more violent against the members of the executive government than his own sentiments and his real political views would, in moments of cool reflection, have permitted him to be. The Abbé Lacordaire did not sound sufficiently the sources of his opinions; M. de Montalembert did not properly measure his attacks. But in spite of their shortcomings and of our own, of their faults and of our own, in all the struggles that grew out of religious questions between us, they rendered constantly faithful and powerful services to their cause, which, notwithstanding our dissentiments on other points, was really the cause of Christ's Faith awaking to new birth and life on the bosom of Liberty.

It is not without well reflecting that I term that *our* cause. When religious liberty reigns in a State, it is a great and a too common error to believe that the statesmen charged with its government have no religious belief whatever; that they are careless in matters of faith because they embrace and advocate the cause of liberty of conscience. The soul does not abdicate the right to its proper and intimate life, because it respects in other souls the rights of that same life; and nothing is more logical or more legitimate than to sustain with fervor the principle of freedom of conscience, and yet to be at the same time a true and an earnest Christian.

I have not here to make a profession of faith for others; but I affirm that, from 1830 to 1848, the Prince whom I had the honor to serve, and the Cabinets to which I had the honor to belong, not only always had at heart the maintenance, however difficult, of the principle of religious liberty, but that they always felicitated themselves upon the progress made by the Christian Faith, even when the manner of that progress was for them a source of serious embarrassment. In 1841 we were placed, in this respect, in a most trying position. Great was the general astonishment, and violent were the attacks made upon us, when, with a devotedness to Catholicism even bolder than had been his conferences at Notre Dame, the Abbé Lacordaire returned from Rome a monk, and a monk of an order which has left more somber memories behind it than any other, that of St. Dominic. This is not the place to examine what the utility may be in our days to the Catholic Church of the monastic orders, or to inquire whether the services they are capable of rendering the Church outweigh the objections and the feelings of repulsion and uneasiness which they arouse. No well-read man can deny their having, in seasons of chaotic confusion, effectually served the cause, not only of the Christian Faith, but of civilization, of science, and even of liberty.

The condition of society and of the human mind is now very different, and the monastic orders cannot take the same position or produce the same effects. But whatever we may think of the opportuneness of their reconstruction, of the right there can be no doubt. Under a system sanctioning freedom of conscience and free institutions, associations for religious purposes cannot be worse treated than those for purposes of industry, commerce, or literature. The State is required to exercise upon combinations of every kind a certain degree of surveillance; but doubtless the union of souls and of lives under one rule and in one costume, with a view to eternal interests, is not a juster cause for disquietude than a union of purses and of labor for the purpose of economizing both, with a view to worldly interests. In 1829, some young Catholic Liberals, MM. de

Carné, de Cazalès, de Champagny, de Montalembert, Foisset de Meaux, Henri Gouraud, founded a periodical, *Le Correspondant*, devoted to the reconciliation of Catholicism with the free social institutions of the age. The *Correspondant* had been suspended in 1835, but reappeared in 1843, under the editorship of M. Charles Lenormant, one of those friends I have lost who retain in my memory the place they occupied in my life. In conducting this work, he kept ever in view the principles in which it had originated, and among other positions, he defended in 1845, with the frank intrepidity both of a Catholic and of a Liberal, the rights of those religious associations which were at the time the object of violent debate.* The cabinet abstained from all measures of repression, and left the new monks freely to their chances of success or failure. Twenty-five years have since

* Des associations religieuses dans le catholicisme; de leur esprit, de leur histoire et de leur avenir; par Charles Lenormant, de l'Institut. Paris: 1845.

elapsed; the Père Lacordaire mounted once more, in his costume as a Dominican, his pulpit in Notre-Dame; he resuscitated in France an order forgotten, or the object of dread only; and to what trouble or embarrassment, I ask, to what complaints even, has this resuscitation led? To what pretensions of ambition have these monks laid claim? what turbulent disposition have they manifested? They have paced meekly along our streets; they have preached eloquently in our churches; they have founded some houses of education; they have made use of their rights as freemen, without offering in any way to infringe the liberty of any other class of citizens. More than all this: the sincerity of their sentiments and language has been put to the proof; the Père Lacordaire resumed, as a Dominican, at Paris, at Toulouse, at Nancy, at Bordeaux, the conferences and the preaching that had rendered him popular as a simple priest; they became, perhaps, more liberal even than they had been originally.

When the tempest of 1848 had given birth, in the imaginations of all men, to every kind of dream, and had opened to every ambition every career, the Père Lacordaire was returned by the popular suffrage as Deputy to the Constituent Assembly. For a moment he thought a new era opening for his Church—perhaps for himself. In this arena, upon which the passions of party were unchained amid the general darkness resting upon society, he soon discovered that the priest and monk of our day was not in his proper place; he withdrew from it to resume, in his modest retreat at Sorèze, his true mission as a Christian teacher. He afterward issued from it, but for a moment only, to express in the French Academy his faith as a Catholic, and his confidence in the democratic principles of modern times. Such are the peaceable, such the only results among us, of the re-establishment of the order of the Dominicans and of the glory of its restorer.

Its *only* results? Not so; if the work of the

Père Lacordaire did not exercise any important influence upon the laity, it was attended with fruitful and salutary effects in the Church of Rome itself. Like him, other priests had the courage to brave the prejudices of the age respecting the religious orders; like him, others refused to suffer themselves to be subjugated by the alarms felt by most members of their Church at the names of Science and of Liberty; and like him, they scrupled not to devote themselves to a common life and a common rule, "to work together," according to their own expressions, "to secure the triumph of Christian truth, and its triumph by means of Philosophy and Science." Thus was re-established, under the direction of the pious curate of Saint-Roch, the Père Pététot, the congregation of the Oratoire—that learned and modest society that gave to France Malebranche and Massillon, and of which Bossuet said, two centuries ago: "The immense love for the Church of the Cardinal de Bérulle inspired him with the design of forming a company, to which he desired to give no other spirit than the very spirit of the Church, no other rule than its canons, no other superiors than its bishops, no other goods than its charity, no other solemn vows than those of baptism and the priesthood. . . . There, to form true priests, they lead them to the fountain of truth; they have always in their hands the sacred volume, to search there unceasingly its literal sense by study, its spirit by prayer, its depth of meaning by retreat from the world, and its end by charity—the termination of everything and the treasure of Christianity—'Christiani nominis thesaurus,' as Tertullian terms it." * Dating its restoration from only thirteen years ago, the new congregation of the Oratoire is still not numerous, and remains little known; it is poor, and it desires to remain so; it has need of extension and of support, but at the very

* Bossuet, Oraison funèbre du père Bourgoing, delivered in 1662, vol. viii, p. 271.

outset of its new career it proved itself faithful to its origin and worthy of the words of Bossuet. One of its founders, the Père Gratry, took his place at once in the first rank of the Christian apologists, moralists, and writers of the day: he is a man at once animated and gentle, full of his peculiar ideas and sentiments, which he carries to an enthusiastic height, but without pride and without jealousy, and ardently propagating them by his books, his lectures, and his conversation. These are all distinguished by eloquent appeals to human sympathies, touching even where they do not convince, and leaving the mind always in emotion at the prospects which they open. Another member of the new Oratoire, the Père Valvoger, has given a succinct account, in a learned work, ("Introduction historique et critique aux livres du Nouveau Testament,") of the Researches and Evidences of Christianity, by the principal foreign theologians. Under the strong influence of the opinions of its first founders, and at the same time comprehending the mind and the requirements of France at the present day, the rising congregation of the Oratoire does not evade examination or discussion; it respects science, and in the religious truths which it teaches, and its relations with the souls that it summons to believe, it does not shrink from accepting fearlessly the terms and the forms of liberty.

In the midst of this great movement of men's minds in matters of religion, what has been done since the opening of this century by the chiefs of the Catholic Church of France, by their bishops and by the clergy, called, by their alliance with the State and by their own rights, to assume the education and the Christian direction of the human soul?

They were at first and especially occupied with the real resuscitation of that Christian religion, now returning to French society, to its rank there and to its mission, but returning as exiles return—ill provided, disorganized, and to a home that seems no home. To render back to France, now Catholic, churches for its worship, priests for its churches, seminaries to form its priests, pupils to people those seminaries; to assure also to the edifice thus rising from its ruins the time for its proper establishment and consolidation—such, under the first empire, was the dominant thought, almost the exclusive thought, of the Episcopacy, of the clergy instituted by the Concordat. A work great and difficult, for which neither materials nor workmen were at hand, and which required for its accomplishment strong support and a long period of repose. The clergy of this epoch have been justly reproached with their uniform obsequiousness to the Emperor Napoleon. No doubt it was a shameful spectacle, in 1811, which those docile bishops afforded, when they assembled in council and were never weary of lavishing caresses upon the despot who had not only stripped the chief of their Church, Pius VII., of his dominions, but was then detaining him a prisoner at Savona, denying his natural counselors, the cardinals, all access to him, refusing him even a secretary to write his letters, and charging an officer of the gendarmerie to watch by day and by night all his movements. Only a single fact explains and somewhat excuses the pusillanimity of the clergy when confronted with this tyranny: these bishops had seen Christianity proscribed, its churches closed, profaned, demolished, its priests hunted and massacred, their flocks left without any worship, any guide, any consolation. The chance of the recurrence of such events filled them with horror. Who could affirm that there was no such chance, and that the reality of the eve was not the possibility of the morrow? With such causes of apprehension a good priest might feel his conscience profoundly troubled; and a timid priest might regard his weakness as justified. What sacrifices were not permissible, nay, even imperative, to prevent such disasters?

Still, the violent measures of Napoleon did not fail to encounter, sometimes rebukes, and occasionally resistance, on the part of the clergy; it was not only that some prelates* in the council, with more courage than moderation, censured his conduct toward the Pope: the council itself—forgetting at last, in its anxiety to vindicate the honor of the whole body, its long habit of obsequiousness—voted an address to the Emperor, an act of independence which occasioned its abrupt dissolution. And of the two ecclesiastics to whose counsels, from just motives of esteem, Napoleon showed least disinclination to give ear, one—the Abbé Émery, "Superior General" of the Congregation of St. Sulpice—had just previously, not long before he died, openly, yet with dignity, resisted the Emperor;† the other, M. Duvoisin, Bishop of

* Among others M. d'Avian, Archbishop of Bordeaux, M. de Boulogne, Bishop of Troyes, and M. de Broglie, Bishop of Gaud.

† Vie de M. Émery, supérieur général du séminaire et de la compagnie de Saint-Sulpice, t. ii, pp. 236–346. Paris: 1862.

Nantes, dictated upon his deathbed these powerful and affectionate lines: "I supplicate the Emperor to restore the holy Father to liberty. His captivity troubles the extreme moments of my life. On several occasions I had the honor to inform the Emperor of the affliction which this captivity is causing to the whole of Christendom, and of the inconveniences which would attend its prolongation. The happiness of his Majesty himself, I believe, depends upon the return of his Holiness to Rome." Idly does Despotism excuse its arbitrary acts, as if they resulted from the want of foresight or the servility of its flatterers; for the blindest have their gleams of light, and even the most timid their intrepid moments, during which they speak the truth, although they speak it in vain.

Under the Restoration, it was no longer fear, but hope—hope ill-founded, too—which misled the French clergy, betrayed them into the commission of many faults, and checked the progress of roused Christendom. In the then reaction against the Revolution, ecclesiastical ambition had its part; partisans of the Crown and of Rome—ardent ones—some through sincere devotion, others from political calculation, believed it to be necessary and possible to restore to the Catholic clergy a part at least of the social position and of the direct authority which they had possessed before 1789. This was evincing a strange ignorance of the fundamental character of French society, such as it has been made by its history and by its great modern Revolution. French society is essentially and insuperably "laic;" the separation of temporals from spirituals, and the empire of the laity in public affairs, are consummated and dominant facts, not to be attacked, or even menaced, without occasioning throughout the whole framework of society an irritation and a disquietude, perilous alike for Church and for State. Nothing in France at the present moment is more fatal to the influence of religion than the chance, or the appearance even, of ecclesiastical domination. This chance and this appearance were, under the Restoration, the plague of the Catholic religion and of the French clergy—a plague the grave consequences of which are the more to be deplored as it was neither very deep-seated nor very formidable. It is a fact too little remarked, that the clergy were not then the principal authors of the faults which subsequently both they and religion had such cause to rue. No doubt many inadmissible claims, many unreasonable and offensive requirements, many rash expectations, proceeded from the ranks of the clergy; but there was in all this more a suggestion of their past history, or an unmeaning vanity, than a real and ardent ambition; even the clergy felt instinctively that political power was not now suited to them, and that France would no longer accept at their hands as ministers even a Cardinal Richelieu or a Cardinal Mazarin. At first the contra-revolutionary and non-ecclesiastical party in the

Chamber of 1815, and, afterward, the blind fanatical coterie of the Court of Charles the Tenth, hurried the clergy into their own vortex, and compromised the cause of religion by making its ministers instruments of their influence and auxiliaries in their combats. The ecclesiastics had not the courage to resist; in spite of their distaste for the new spirit which was abroad, most of the bishops and of the priesthood, warned by their experience in the Revolution, would have preferred to remain out of the sphere of politics, and to confine themselves to the functions of their religious mission, rather than to be constantly struggling against popular opinions; so, when any opportunity presented itself to show their sympathy, they hastened to embrace it. When, in 1824, the bill of M. de Villèle for the conversion of the "Rentes" created a great stir among the "Bourgeoisie" of Paris, it was the Archbishop of Paris, M. de Quélen, who constituted himself in the Chamber of Peers the principal organ of the Opposition; and when, in 1828, the movement of public opinion and of the magistracy against the religious congregations wrested from the King (Charles the Tenth) the Ordonnances of the 21st June, the Bishop of Beauvais, M. Feutries, at that time the Minister of Ecclesiastical Affairs, did not hesitate to countersign them. The members of the priesthood live in close contact with the people, and cannot long remain in ignorance of the real state of their opinions, or long persist in holding them lightly. The French clergy, as a whole, were more resigned to the new state of society than King Charles the Tenth and his intimate friends; the false ideas and the unreasonable political pretensions of the monarch and of the coterie which formed his court, far more than the religious bigotry of the Church, occasioned the great faults committed under the Restoration.

At all epochs and in all parties some man is always met with in whom are centered and personified whatever good sense, sound views, and wise purposes there are in the party to which he belongs. Such a man under the Restoration and for the lay Legitimists was M. de Villèle. True to his friends, he nevertheless knew, or I should rather say he promptly learned in public life to understand, what France then actually was, and what qualities, to be successful, her government should possess. If he had had toward his party and his king as much independence and firmness in action as he had correct appreciation in thought, he might perhaps have obtained a more complete and more lasting success. The clergy on their side also had at this epoch a faithful representative of whatever religious or political sagacity existed in the French Church: it is here to the Abbé Frayssinous, Bishop of Hermopolis, that the honor and the merit belong. His task was far easier than that of M. de Villèle, for he was never put to any trial: he had no struggle to sustain; he remained naturally, or kept himself voluntarily, out of the arena of events and of parties; but it was in this precisely that he showed his good sense, and his correct appreciation of the permanent interests and the real dispositions of the clergy of his time. Neither as theologian, nor as orator, nor as statesman was the Abbé Frayssinous a man of eminence, or remarkable for power of intellect; but in the different phases of his career, in his personal conduct, and in his writings, he had an unerring instinct of what was just and possible, and showed no common tact in retiring with dignity from untenable positions, and escaping from questions that he could not settle. Upon these occasions he would confine himself to his mission of a priest and moralist of the Christian religion. From 1803 to 1822 he held, suspended, and resumed in the Church of St. Sulpice, his "conferences upon religious subjects;" remarkable not only by a judicious defense of the great truths of Christianity, but by a continuous, although somewhat timorous, effort to place the

6

doctrines of the Church in harmony with the principles of natural justice and of civil liberty. He was not, like the Père Lacordaire or M. de Montalembert, a Catholic Liberal; he was a priest—moderate and equitable, not from lukewarmness in his faith, but from respect to legal rights and human sentiments. Although his "conferences" had not the success and popularity that distinguished later, in Nôtre-Dame, those of the Père Lacordaire, they attracted a numerous auditory, and exercised material influence in giving to the awakening of Christianity a wider range and a firmer basis.* In his work upon the true principles of the Gallican Church, the Abbé Frayssinous manifested the same moderate and conciliatory spirit—not

* The "conferences" of the Abbé Frayssinous at St. Sulpice have been published under this title: Défense du Christianisme, ou conférences sur la religion. 3 vols. 8vo. Paris: 1825. The Abbé Frayssinous published also in 1818 a work with the following title: Les vrais principes de l'église gallicane sur la puissance ecclesiastique, la Papauté, les Libertés gallicanes, la Promotion des évêques, les trois Concordats, et les Appels comme d'abus.

always tracing principles to their sources, but never pushing facts or ideas to their extreme consequences; while remaining the faithful servant of the Church he showed himself also rather the friend of Christian peace than the jealous advocate of ecclesiastical power. His mode of life was as modest as his opinions; he never made power his aim, neither did he ever seek for honors, whether political, ecclesiastical, or academic; he declined them even when within his reach. He joined the Cabinet in 1824, as Minister of Ecclesiastical Affairs and of Public Instruction; he withdrew from it in 1828, when the mounting wave of Liberalism demanded that a more vigorous policy should be adopted against the religious congregations than the pupil and orator of St. Sulpice was willing to sanction. He neither had the qualities necessary for governing the French clergy, nor did he pretend to govern them; but he represented them, nevertheless, in all their more irreproachable and prudent opinions. Unfortunately, mere common sense and prudence do not suffice more in the Church than in the State to save nations from the consequences of their faults of omission and commission; for this object, higher qualities are necessary as well as more rude efforts.

It was one of the first effects of the Revolution in 1830, to make visible to all the injury that the faults of their friends, rather than the blows of their adversaries, had inflicted, under the Restoration, upon the clergy, and through the clergy upon religion. The acts of violence which, during the revolutionary crisis from 1830 to 1832, were directed at the Churches—the crosses thrown down, the insulting cries, and antichristian manifestations; a little later, the riot before the church of St. Germain l'Auxerrois, on the occasion of the service celebrated on the anniversary of the death of the Duke de Berri—the archiepiscopal palace ruined and pillaged—the church broken into and closed—the menaces directed at the priests—what were all these deplorable acts but the explosion of a popular reaction, provoked by the share a part of the clergy had taken in favor of a retrograde policy—of a return to the ancient régime and to absolutism? Violent men profited by this reaction to satisfy their impiety and licentiousness, but they could never have excited the movement or made it successful had they hoisted their own banner; there must be some little truth before a populace will suffer itself to be so misled; and the crowd who in February, 1831, so furiously rose in insurrection before St. Germain l'Auxerrois, would have paused in astonishment had it perceived that what it was so brutally attacking and destroying was—not the ancient régime, not absolutism—but religion and liberty.

To put an end to this confusion, full at once of deception and of peril, but a single thing was required: to banish from the Church, and from its relations with the State, worldly ambition and influences, and to replace them by influences of a moral description; instead of a political banner, they should have only hoisted the banner of religious faith and liberty of conscience. That was the great work, or, to use a better expression, the great progress, which from 1830 to 1848 was aimed at and accomplished.

The efforts made and the debates instituted at this epoch by the most eminent champions of the Church are remarkable, because they no longer proposed to restore any fragment of its ancient power, but to insure to it its place and its share in the new public institutions of liberty. The little militant party of Catholic Liberals quitted the arena of the ancient political régime, and took up their position on that of the new constitution, claiming for the Church, for its ministers, and for its faithful subjects, the exercise of all the rights and the free development of all the power that, under the constitution, either belonged, or ought to belong, to all citizens. They made no reservation of opinion, no effort more or less covert, in furtherance of any pretensions of bygone times, whether dynastic, aristrocratic, or theocratic; the frank acceptance of the present age and actual society, provided that Christian faith, Christian morals, and Christian institutions, might have free room to work; such was, in the midst of all the factions and political plottings of this period, the constant attitude of the Catholic Liberal party, that is, of M. de Montalembert, the Père Lacordaire, M. Charles Lenormant, Frederic Ozanam, and of the friends in small number grouped around them.

Whoever feels astonished that their number was so small, shows little acquaintance with our country or our times. The enterprise which they undertook was singularly bold and difficult; to drag France out of its rut of incredulity and irreligion, and at the same time to extricate Catholicism from its rut of impolicy, its alliance with absolutism, its timorous immobility in the presence of liberty; to proclaim and simultaneously to defend, in spirituals, the Christian faith, and, in temporals, the régime of liberty. Certainly in France, and in the 19th century, the devotion of men to such a task supposes an enthusiasm and an energy of conviction of which few are capable; and if the new Christian Liberals flattered themselves that success would be easy, events must soon have disabused them. Attacked with ardor by the opponents of all religion, they were also assailed by Catholics devoted to the ancient régime of the Church, and alarmed at the new system pressed upon their acceptance. The former of these two attacks caused the Catholic Liberals neither surprise nor embarrassment; but the latter brought with it bitter annoyance and disappointment, for they found directly opposed to them members of their own faith. Soon they were to have as their adversary a man who, by his vigorous talents—employed with equal violence against the incredulous of all shades of opinions, and against the Catholic Liberals too—exercised an influence upon a great number of Catholics, whether of the laity or priesthood, and indisposed them to any reconciliation with that modern society which he irritated still more against them. I knew M. Veuillot at the commencement of his literary career, when he accompanied General Bugeaud to the seat of his government in Algeria. At this epoch he addressed to me two memorials upon the subject of the moral condition of the colony and of the army. They struck me by their decided tone, and the straightforwardness and candor with which he expressed sentiments already distinguished by devotion. Already he regarded the religion of his own Church, and of *it* alone, as the sure basis of human morality and social order; but he had not yet proclaimed as his doctrine the deplorable error that Faith enjoins war upon Liberty. He merited a better understanding of the cause of Christianity; he merited to be a better advocate of the Church at Rome than an advocate who, although one of its most devoted defenders, has yet most injured the cause that he sought to serve.

These political revolutions and these domestic dissensions left, in the period that ensued after 1830, the Catholic Church in a difficult situation, but in one salutary for it and fruitful of consequences. The clergy no longer counted on the favor of Government, but they had at the same time to fear from it neither violence nor hostility. Left to themselves, they felt the necessity of independent existence, and saw that they must replace credit with the authorities by influence with the country; and this influence they were likely to obtain. If they did not possess all the privileges which they coveted, they had enough to enable them every day to conquer additional powers, supposing them willing and sagacious enough to take the trouble and employ the right means. In my opinion, they did not do at this epoch, in the interest of religion and of the Church, all that their position permitted, or all that their mission required at their hands; but temporal or spiritual governors, layman or priests, who ever did, I do not say what he ought, but what he could have done? The greater part of the bishops and of the priests were vacillating and timorous; the problem before them went beyond their opinions, and the events beyond their strength; the impetuous Liberalism of M. de Montalembert and of his friends disquieted them; they saw in him rather a valiant champion than a representative they could rely upon. Among those who joined with him in the struggle for the freedom of instruction, there were some who showed, with reference to the Government of 1830 and the University, little fairness or prudence: these injured the cause rather than served it. Whether from submission to orders from Rome, or from their natural impulse, the clergy, taken as a whole, showed little taste for liberty; even while they demanded it, they were rather inclined to immobility than progress. But whatever the fears and hesitations of individuals, when the general current of ideas and of popular opinions once penetrates to the classes least disposed to entertain them, it never fails, whether they avow it, or whether they even know it, to swell and to advance. Around and among the clergy themselves the spirit of progress and of liberty gained ground, although by insensible degrees. Here and there individual priests, like the Abbé Bautain, formerly a student with M. Jouffroy at the École Normale, and Professor of Philosophy in the Faculty of Letters at Strasbourg, propagated in the Church the liberal movement, forming for it in different places new centers of action. The spirit which had awakened Christianity manifested itself, too, in our great lay establishments for the higher course of instruction; not always without check, but still with a success the more conspicuous the more it was contested. In 1846, some disturbances, occasioned by a thoughtless and puerile intolerance, made by M. Lenormant, at that time my substitute (suppléant) in the chair of Modern History at the Faculty of Letters, determine to withdraw from the Sorbonne, where he had made a courageous avowal of his faith; but M. Ozanam, the worthy successor to the chair of M. Fauriel, maintained in the same place the same principles with a more successful perseverance, and with such a depth of conviction and such a warmth of emotion that sometimes he carried the feelings of his auditors away with him, and sometimes commanded respectful attention even from those most confirmed in their incredulity. And while the spirit of Christianity was thus manifesting itself in the free Faculty of Letters, the teaching of the Faculty of Theology attested, under that same roof, a notable progress in knowledge and in Liberalism. The Abbé Maret, in his lectures on the Dogmas of Religion, the Abbé Frère, in his discourses on the Scriptures; the Abbé Dupanloup and the Abbé Gerbet, in their lectures on Sacred Eloquence, displayed not only a firm and active faith, but views upon philosophy, history, and literature, necessarily implying an aquaintance with the works of human science, and an appreciation of the rights of liberty. Ecclesiastics and laymen, not members of the scientific establishments of the State, published, under the name of the "Université Catholique," a series of courses in which philosophy, history, natural sciences, archæology, and the arts were explained and taught in harmony with the dogmas and sentiments of religious men. And even far from Paris, in several great episcopal seminaries, classical and theological studies took a wider range, and attained a scientific value that they had not for a long time possessed.

"Faith, if it hath not works, is dead, being alone," says the Apostle St. James. Christianity has borne abundant fruits since its awakening at the commencement of this century. I have before me the "Manual des Œuvres et institutions de charité de Paris," published in 1862, by order of the archbishop, M. Sibour. Independently of the establishments under the direction of Government, I find in it 107 charitable institutions or associations, of every kind, originated and supported by zealous Christians in the interval between 1820 and 1848. Of these I will only cite some of the principal ones, to establish their character and their progress. In the year 1822 the idea struck two poor servants at Lyons to make the rounds of their parish and collect weekly one sou from each person, in aid of the conversion of infidels. This was the origin of the association called "l'Œuvre de la propagation de la Foi," now under the direction of two councils, composed of members of the clergy and of the laity, having their sittings, one at Lyons, the other at Paris. The report published by this association in June, 1824, showed for the two years, 1823 and 1824, a receipt of 80,000 fr., (3200*l.*) This association received in 1864 the sum of 5,090,041 fr. 48 cent., (203,601*l.* 13*s.* 3½*d.*,) in which amount France alone figures for

3,479,290 fr. 65 cent., (139,171*l.* 12*s.* 6½*d.*,) and it divided 4,658,672 fr. 56 cent. (186,346*l.* 18*s.* 6½*d.*) among five hundred dioceses, and appropriated those funds to the support of the Catholic missionaries in the five parts of the world. It counted from the year 1852, 1,500,000 subscribers, and it distributed 170,000 copies of its "Annals," (Annales de propagation de la Foi,) which form a sequel to the "Lettres édificantes," and keep the Christian world informed of their doings. In May, 1833, eight young men, at the suggestion of Frederic Ozanam, "wishing," said the Perè Lacordaire, "to give one more proof of what Christianity can effect in behalf of the poor, began to ascend to those upper stories which were the hidden haunts of the misery of their quarter. Men saw youths in the flower of their age and fresh from school regularly visiting, without any feeling of repulsion, the most abject habitations, and conveying to their unknown and suffering tenants a passing vision of charity." Twenty years later, in

1853, Ozanam said at Florence, when on his death-bed: "Instead of eight only, at Paris alone we are two thousand strong, and we visit five thousand families, that is to say, about twenty thousand individuals, or a quarter of the poor contained in that great city. The conferences in France alone number five hundred, and we have them too in England, in Spain, Belgium, America, and even in Jerusalem." Nine years afterward, in 1862, when the Government, listening to mistaken counsels, suppressed the General Council of the Conferences of St. Vincent de Paul, and by doing so destroyed the central bond that kept the society together, the latter counted more than 3000 local conferences; it consisted of about 30,000 members, who visited in their homes more than 100,000 indigent families, and had already introduced into the greater part of the principal cities a system which exercised a control over the interests of apprentices and of prisoners. During the course of the same epoch the Sisters of Charity, whose number, a century after their foundation by St. Vincent de Paul, had not exceeded 1500, already reached 18,000, of whom 16,000 were Frenchwomen; and at this moment they are plying throughout the world their works of piety and charity. Another society, "Les petites sœurs des pauvres," was founded in 1845, in imitation of Jeanne Jugan, a poor servant, a native of Brittany, who had been just crowned by the French Academy. This society receives and succors in their establishment nearly 20,000 aged men. Another association, "Les Frères de la doctrine Chrétienne," which had in the year 1844, 468 schools, maintains this year (1865) 920, and the number of the pupils has increased from 198,188 to 335,382. State and ecclesiastical documents attest, that by concurring causes of encouragement on the part of the State, of local subventions and of private donations, ten thousand churches have been, during the last fifty years, built, rebuilt, or suitably adapted for the performance of the services of the Church of Rome. I might cite many similar facts. In all the directions and under all the forms in which piety and charity manifest themselves, faith and liberty, and faith and science have, since the awakening of Christianity and since the cause of religion has been separated from politics, drawn nearer to one another, and faith and its manifestation by charity have made a simultaneous advance and a like progress.

Had the Government of 1830 remained standing; had State and Church each retained reciprocally the same situation and the same attitude, the facts to which I have just alluded might have long remained unobserved. Society does not, any more than individuals, render an account to itself of the intimate relations of its existence, or of the transformations to which these give rise; but Providence has its moments when it suddenly lightens up the stage of the world and reveals to all actors and spectators the import and the effect of what is passing around them. The Revolution of 1848 threw upon the progress of the Catholic Church and its relations with French society since 1830 the clear light of such a revelation.

In this sudden subversion of all things, in the presence of a republic extemporized upon the ruins of three monarchies—the monarchy of glory, the monarchy of tradition, and the monarchy of public opinion—in the midst of this nation, suddenly insurgent and beyond either its aim or expectation sovereign, what became of the Church? What did its ministers? If some of them participated in the current dreams, certainly the majority were full of anguish and alarm; they did not combat the new institutions; they did not pretend to exercise any influence for or against any party; they sought only to purify the Republic by securing in it a place for Religion; they did not stand aloof from the people; they showed themselves, in its great assemblages and in its fêtes, planting the cross of Jesus by the side of the tree of liberty. Never did the Church stand so aloof from politics; never was she more modest in her attitude; never less exacting—I will not say more obsequious, as far as the Government or the public was concerned; never more absorbed with her mission of piety and morality, whatever the Government of France might be, and whoever her masters.

And what in their turn was the conduct of the people toward the Church? I do not mean to say that they confided in her, or showed her much affection. The popular movement in 1848 was no doubt far from being religious; and the ideas, acts, and language which proceeded from it every instant, were well calculated to disturb and sadden the hearts of Christians; but religion and its ministers were in no respect ill treated, insulted, or persecuted; their forms of worship were not interrupted: when they showed themselves out of doors, they were received with respect; and at the sight of a virtuous archbishop mortally wounded in the streets, in the very endeavor to appease the civil war by the exhibition of the cross, a painful stupor seized the people; a pang of remorse and of shame traversed those masses of disbelievers at the sight of a martyr. It was clear that in the interval between 1830 and 1848, although the Christian Church had not aroused in the people either faith or sympathy, that Church had at least won liberty and peace.

When the revolutionary fever had subsided, when the Republic had given itself a chief, and was waiting for a master, it was no longer in the street, by popular impressions, but in the Assemblies, and by the constituted authorities, that the great questions of the day were put and were solved. There, too, the progress, which the Catholic Church had made, became immediately evident, and its gains were ascertained. It counted at this moment among its most zealous servants a man new to public affairs, who had entered political life as an adherent of the Legitimist Opposition to the

Monarchy of 1830, a man who accepted the Republic, and had acquired in a few days a just renown by his courageous resistance to anarchy. By a choice, fortunate but at the same time unforeseen, M. de Falloux became the Minister of Public Instruction and of Worship in the first cabinet formed by the Prince President of the Republic. The new minister immediately devoted himself to the important measure that the Catholic Church had had in view ever since the year 1830, that is, to the complete establishment, under the sanction of the law, of the principle of liberty of instruction. He proceeded in his task at once with intelligence and boldness. To prepare his project of law, he appointed a numerous commission, and summoned to it the most eminent men, who represented views and interests the most diverse; laymen and ecclesiastics, Romanists, Protestants and philosophers, Republicans, Legitimists, Orleanists and Bonapartists, M. Thiers and the Abbé Dupanloup, M. Cousin and M. de Montalembert, M. Saint

Marc Girardin and M. Cochin, M. Cuvier and the Abbé Sibour.*

M. Thiers was the president of this commission, which sat during five months. It discussed every question respecting the organization of public instruction with a passionate ardor, and, at the same time, with an earnest and sincere desire to conciliate, by their resolutions, all opinions. According to the character of the times and the state of public sentiment, critical and perilous situations precipitate men sometimes to the commission of insane acts of violence, and sometimes keep them within the line of fairness and prudence. The project of law which issued from the commission of M. de Falloux had the merit of prudence. In

* The following is a complete list of the members of the Commission, as given in the "Moniteur" of the 22d June, 1849: M. Thiers, president; MM. Cousin, St. Marc Girardin, Dubois, the Abbé Dupanloup, Peupin, Janvier, Laurentie, Freslon, Ballaguet, de Montalembert, Fresneau, Poulain de Bossay, Cuvier, Michel, Armand de Melun, Henri de Riancey, Cochin, the Abbé Sibour, Roux-Lavergne, de Montreuil-Housset, and Alexis Chevalier, secretary.

making mutual concessions, the representatives of the different systems took good care to protest that they did not renounce their peculiar principles—a language which made sometimes their resolutions have the air of a superficial and incoherent compromise; but men could, nevertheless, observe how conspicuous that project was for its large and practical character, and its respect for different rights; and they could also see how the State, the Church, and private establishments were left free to compete in matters of public instruction. When this project was discussed in the Legislative Assembly, M. de Falloux was no longer minister; but the impulse had been given, and his measure was out of danger; his successor, M. de Parien, too, gave it the support which it deserved; and after a discussion which occupied thirty-seven sittings, the Assembly, by a strong majority, passed the law, without introducing any important modification. The Liberty of Instruction was founded.

Fifteen years have passed, and it subsists. The State, the Church, private institutions founded by laymen or by ecclesiastics, have competed actively during all that period. Religious congregations, Lazarists, Dominicans, Oratorians, Jesuits, have in this struggle displayed all the enthusiasm of faith, all the ardor of reciprocal rivalry. The Jesuits, since the year 1850, have opened twenty colleges for secondary instruction, and have founded at Paris, for courses of study preparatory to the special schools, an establishment whose successes have attracted the attention of the government and of the public; for it sends every year to the Military Schools, the Polytechnic, Naval, or Central, an extraordinary number of successful candidates, who have passed with honor, although the competition has been extensive and the examinations are severe. A great school, founded by the Archbishop of Paris for the higher branches of ecclesiastical study in the ancient house of the Carmelites, has formed priests who, in the public examinations and theses, have proved themselves capable of taking rank by the side of the best pupils of the lay establishment of the "École Normale Supérieure." Everywhere the University has encountered numerous and ardent rivals; and it has been at the same time in its own interior a prey to painful trials. Under the pretext of an interest for studies of a scientific and practical nature, classical and philosophical studies have been displaced and depreciated. At the very moment that the University was losing its privileges beyond, it saw its principles and its organization shaken inside its walls.

Faithful to her convictions and traditions, even while accepting the experiments and the struggles that were forced upon her, the University has surmounted perils from within and rivalries from without; on the one side, little by little, it has returned to its system of a large and solid teaching of the classics; on the other, the level of the studies in its principal establishments has been raised, and the number of its pupils has been ever on the increase. The Lycées counted (in 1850) 19,300; they have now (1865) more than 30,000 pupils. The State has thrown open the career of instruction to the Church, and has at the same time redoubled its own solicitude and success. Liberty of instruction has calmed both the anxieties of the religious party that made them demand it, and those anxieties of the laity which that liberty had inspired. It has given peace to the State and to the Church, at the same time that it has excited their emulation and stimulated their progress.

An incident which made some noise at the time has, under the new régime, shown the force of the Liberal spirit, and proved that, when needed, it would have unforeseen defenders. Under the influence of a blind zeal, a pious ecclesiastic, the Abbé Gaume, demanded by what right the literature of pagan antiquity occupied the place it did in public teaching;

denounced it as "the devouring canker of modern societies;" and insisted that the Christian classics should replace in our schools the Greek and Latin classics. What was this but to reject one of the great cradles of modern civilization; to condemn the renaissance of literature in the fifteenth century, as well as the religious reform in the sixteenth century; and to close to the minds of rising generations of Christians the general history of the world! This attack upon the system of public instruction which had been in vigor during the last four centuries in all the States of Christendom, met from a part of the Romanists with a sympathetic reception: bishops, eminent for learning, thanked its author; M. Veuillot constituted himself his champion. But in the Catholic Church itself, as well as in the University, the fire of the defense silenced that of the attack; ecclesiastics, as eminent by their piety as by their science, the Bishop of Orleans at their head, proclaimed aloud their sympathy for the comprehensive scheme and the liberal studies which embrace all the fair works of man's intelligence. The Jesuits on this occasion set an example of broad views and common sense; they introduced no modification into the programmes of their colleges; the Pères Cahoux and Daniel demonstrated their propriety, nay, their necessity; and the literature of the Greeks and of the Romans has preserved in the education of Christians the place which it gained in their history by the right of genius and by the splendor of its productions.

Scarcely had this controversy on a literary and moral subject been settled, when questions of far more gravity were raised, and more profoundly agitated Christian society. Christians found themselves attacked simultaneously upon scientific and upon political grounds. Men denied to the Christian Faith its reasonableness and its vital sources—to the Church of Rome its traditional and historical régime, and the temporal power of its chief.

Two things strike me in this double attack—on the one hand its timidity, yet gravity; on the other, the powerful resistance which it encounters. Nothing is less novel than a denial of the supernatural character of Christianity, and of its primitive facts, of its miracles, of the divinity of its founder. The eighteenth century carried on this war in a far more violent, rude, and iniquitous spirit than the nineteenth century has done. M. Renan, in the attempt to dethrone Jesus, has at least treated him with admiration and respect; not from calculation, I feel assured, but from the natural tone of his mind. In our time, men have instincts and tastes, at once inconsequent and prudent; at the very time when they engage in a deadly struggle they affect to carry thither the cool impartiality of spectators; they flatter themselves that they unite the acumen of the critic to the feeling of the poet. The skeptic shows no disinclination to play the mystic; and the erudite man strives to cover with the vail of fancy the ruin that he makes. Hume was a more stubborn skeptic, and Voltaire an enemy more daring. If I pass from philosophy to politics, and from books to events, I observe the war undergoing a similar transformation. What a contrast between the attacks of the Directory and the Emperor Napoleon the First upon the Papacy, and the circumspect and hesitating treatment of which, in spite of the blows that it receives, the Papacy is in these days the object? Are we to conclude that the general course of events has changed, and that the flood, which for a century whirled Europe along, is arrested and subsiding? Certainly not: there are abundant facts to prove the contrary. Whether regarded as a religious or a political question, whether considered as affecting opinions or interests, the contest between authority and liberty, between faith and incredulity, is carried on more earnestly and more systematically now than ever: principles on each side are pushed to their extreme consequences, and contrasted in a manner never before the case. But experience imposes a restraint upon men even where it does not change them. In the years of internal order which the Empire insured, and in the years of liberty to which the constitutional Monarchy gave the sanction of its laws, the different parties learned to appreciate the obstacles with which they had to contend, and to measure their own strength and that of their opponents: they now know that everything is not possible to them; and necessity has inculcated a certain amount of equity and good sense. The experience of the past, as well as that of each day, convinces them of their inability to insure a complete success to their systems and their designs. Its adversaries thought Christianity expiring; but they soon saw that it was still full of life: while they express their surprise and persevere in their warfare, they admit its practical influence, render homage to its moral value, and strive, although they contest its rights, to appropriate to themselves the inheritance of its blessings. The wind has often blown from the right quarter for Catholic Absolutists during this century; they have enjoyed the favor of more than one master, and more than once they have requited him by devoted services. More than once, also, they have obtained from the supreme head of their Church official declarations, which have been used by them against the Catholic Liberals. The Absolutists, nevertheless, have not succeeded in changing the tendency of Christian societies; they have arrested the course neither of ideas nor events; their defeats have cost them dearer than their victories were worth; and in spite of the obstinate infatuation of parties, I doubt whether they themselves believe in the progress of their cause. And how often has the Papacy itself in our days been insulted and despoiled? Has it not even been vanquished and expelled? Still, in spite of what it has suffered, sometimes from revolutions, sometimes from arbitrary power, it has outlived not only the triumphs of its enemies, but its own impolitic measures: and at this day, assailed by freethinkers in spirituals, by ambitious neighbors in temporals, menaced with abandonment even by its protectors, it is more energetically defended and efficaciously supported than it ever was at the commencement of this century in its reverses. Pius VII. never received such pecuniary contributions as have been forwarded to Pius IX. in his necessities; and if the French bishops were now summoned to a council, their conduct would, beyond doubt, be more dignified and more influential than was that of their predecessors in 1811.

Why such changes in a situation itself in effect unchanged? Whence these hesitating measures, this embarrassed attitude of the adversaries of the Christian faith and of the Christian Church? What cause at the same time gives such boldness and even success to their defenders?

Each age has its own peculiar and characteristic mission, and one from which it cannot escape; every human being has his share in it, whether he knows it or not. As a consequence of the truths and the errors, of the good and evil, of the triumphs and reverses of the preceding centuries, the nineteenth century has before it a special task, which will employ all its energies, and which will also, I hope, constitute its glory. It has both in the State and in the Church found the two supreme forces that preside over man's life, and over that of society, Authority and Liberty, in violent conflict, in turn intoxicated with victory, or vanquished, ruined. It is the mission of the nineteenth century to make them live together, and live in peace; or at least in an antagonism entailing upon neither any mortal danger. The recognition of, and respect for, authority; the acceptance and guarantee of freedom; these are the imperative necessities which our age is called upon to feel and to satisfy, both in State and

Church. Nor does this imply, as is often pretended, any inconsistency or any compromise of principle or any policy of expedients; it is not by inconsistency that great questions are settled, it is not by expedients that we content the cravings of men's souls, or calm the anxieties of human society; for mankind yields genuine submission and feels real confidence only where it believes in the existence of truth and justice. The recognition, veneration, and guarantee of the different rights which co-exist naturally and necessarily in human societies—of the rights, both of individuals and of the State—of the rights of religious society and of civil society—of the rights of little local societies as well as of the grand general society—of the rights of conscience as well as of tradition—of the rights of the future as well as of those of the past—these are the dominant principles of which the nineteenth century has to insure the triumph. Triumphs assured, if Liberals and Christians are both of them determined to accomplish it! Notwithstanding all the violent emotions of party, and of all our differences on intellectual and social subjects, the consciousness of this situation is ever before our minds; and whether we admit it or not, the alliance of the liberal movement with the movement of awakened Christianity, is the grand measure and the grand hope of the day.

A Catholic priest, now a bishop, inquiring the origin of the actual disputes of religion, and their probable issue, expresses himself as follows:—"Free institutions, freedom of conscience, political liberty, civil liberty, individual liberty, liberty of families, of education, and of opinions, equality before the laws, the equal division of imposts and of public charges, these are all points upon which we make no difficulty; we accept them frankly; we appeal to them on solemn occasions of public discussion; we accept, we invoke the principles and the liberties proclaimed in 1789; even those who combat those principles and those liberties admit that liberty of religion and free education have become acknowledged, self-evident truths—(*des verités de bon sens*)." *

This Catholic, this bishop, is no timorous priest, disposed to make every sacrifice for the purpose of conciliation. It is the same priest, who, from the first attack made upon the constitution of the Catholic Church, has always distinguished himself by the warmth and ability with which he has defended it. The Papacy, its rights, its temporal independence and spiritual sovereignty never had a champion more resolute, more opposed to weak concessions or fallacious compromises, more constantly intrépid in the breach than the Bishop of Orleans.

When the contest was warmest, the Pope (Pius IX.) published his "Encyclical" of the 8th of December, 1864. Exempt from every feeling of prejudice and hostility, and having no connection or relation with the Papacy to

* De la Pacification religieuse. By the Abbé Dupanloup, pp. 263, 294, 306. Paris, 1845.

make me pause, I feel no hesitation in saying what I think of this document, at once the occasion and the pretext for such a stir. In my opinion the error was a grave one. Regarded as doctrine, the "Encyclical" was dignified and yet embarrassed, positive and yet evasive; it confounded in the same sweeping condemnation salutary truths and pernicious errors, the principles of liberty and the maxims of licentiousness; it made an effort to maintain, in point of right, the ancient traditions and pretensions of Rome, without avowing in point of fact that the ideas and potent influences of modern civilization were the objects of its declared and unceasing hostility. In a system like that of the present day—a system of publicity and freedom of discussion—this manner of proceeding, its inconsistencies, its reticence, its obscurities, whether arising from instinct or premeditation, have ceased to be good policy, and in fact serve no purpose whatever. As a measure to meet a particular emergency, the "Encyclical" of the

8th of December 1864 did not resemble that of Gregory XVI. in 1832; it was not called for by such extravagances as those of the *Avenir*, or those of the Abbé de la Mennais; no urgent necessity, no public exigency required that Rome should pronounce itself; the debate between the Catholic Absolutists and the Catholic Liberals was of ancient date, and was evidently destined to long duration; the Papacy could not flatter itself that it could put an end to this contest by any peremptoriness of decision; her indulgent consideration was as due to the one party as to the other. Doubtless the Catholic Liberals had not shown less zeal for her cause, nor had the services which they had rendered been less important; it was not a moment of peril for Rome, and Rome was bound in justice, without any open declaration at least, to maintain toward them an attitude of reserve. The party, even before the publication of the "Encyclical," had earned, as it still merits, her gratitude and her esteem; neither M. de Montalembert, nor the Prince Albert de Broglie, nor M. de Falloux, nor M. Cochin, nor any of their friends had imitated the example of the Abbé de la Mennais; nor has one of them shown subsequently any irritation, or even uttered a word of complaint; they have maintained a respectful silence. The Bishop of Orleans has done even more. A man of action as well as of faith, he thought in the midst of the storm excited by the "Encyclical" of the 8th of December, that he was bound to consider the perils rather than the faults, and that it became a priest who had supported liberty to support authority also when the object of attack. He threw himself into the arena to cover the Papacy at all hazards with his valiant arms: after having played the part of a sagacious counselor, he played that of a faithful champion, and he inflicted upon her adversaries blows so sturdy, that the latter were in their turn obliged to put themselves upon their defense, even in the midst of the success that the "Encyclical" had insured them.

The Bishop of Orleans is probably reserved for many other struggles; he may even be hurried by a warlike temperament to carry the war into a field where it is uncalled for; but I shall be both surprised and grieved if he do not always remain what he is at this moment in the Church of France, the most enlightened representative of its mission, moral and social, as well as the most intrepid defender of its true and legitimate interests.

Whether the matter in debate concerns religious or social affairs and contests, parties are liable to two errors of equal gravity: they may misapprehend their respective perils, or their respective strength. Wisdom consists in a just appreciation of these perils and of these forces, and it is upon such an appreciation precisely that success itself depends. The actual perils to which Catholicism is exposed are evident to all. It owes its development and its constitution to times essentially different from the present. It adapts itself with reluctance to the principles required and the demands made upon it in this age. Its antagonists think and assert that it will never so adapt itself. Most of the lookers-on, who are indifferent or vacillating—and their number is great—incline to believe its antagonists in the right. This is the trial through which Catholicism is at this moment passing. To pass through it triumphantly, it has two great forces to rely upon; the one is, the reaction in favor of religion occasioned by the follies and the crimes of the Revolution, the other is, the liberal movement that took place among the Catholics after the faults of the Restoration, and the new opening made for them by the Government of 1830. The Concordat built up again the edifice of the Catholic Church; Liberalism is laboring to penetrate its sanctuary, and, without impairing its faith, to obtain for it once more the sympathies of civil government. Let sincere Catholics reflect well upon their course, for here is their main stay, here their best chance for the future; let them maintain with a firm hand the strong constitution of their Church, but accept frankly, and at once claim, their share also in the liberties of their age; let them take care of their anchors and spread their sails, for this is the conduct prescribed to them by the supreme interest, which should be their law, the future interests, I mean, of Christianity.

The time has been short, but the experiment has been made and is successful. I have now enumerated the principal events connected with religion which have taken place in the course of this century in the bosom of the Catholic Church of France. In spite of the obstacles, the oscillations, the deviations, and the faults that are remarkable, the awakening of Christianity is evident. Under the influence of the causes which I have pointed out, Christian faith has evidently made progress; Christian science, progress; Christian charity, as shown by works, progress; Christian force, progress; progress incomplete and insufficient but still progress, real, and full of fruit, symptomatic of vital energy and future promise. Let not the enemies of Christianity deceive themselves; they are waging a combat of life and of death, but their antagonist is not in extremis!

II. AWAKENING OF CHRISTIANITY IN FRANCE.

I PASS without any transitional stage from the awakening of Christianity in the Roman Catholic Church to the awakening of Christianity in the Protestant Church. What need of a transition? I am not quitting the Christian Church. With respect to their claims as Christians, Protestant nations have been put to the test. They have had, like Catholic nations, to pass through violent struggles, to combat evil tendencies, to undergo perilous trials; but the peculiar characteristic of Christianity, the simultaneous action of faith and of science, of authority and liberty, has received a glorious development in the bosom of Protestant nations. England and Holland, Protestant Germany, Sweden, Denmark, Switzerland, and the United States of America, have had their vices, their crimes, their sufferings, and their reverses; but, after all, these States have in the last four centuries labored with effect at the solution, in a Christian sense, of that grand problem of human society—the moral and physical progress of the masses, as well as the political guarantee of their rights and liberties. And in these days the States to which I have alluded resist effectually the shocks—now of anarchy, now of despotism, which alternately trouble the peace of Christendom. As for the Christian Faith itself, if, in Protestant countries, it does not escape the attacks elsewhere made upon it, neither is it without its powerful defenders and faithful followers. In those countries, Christian Churches are full of adherents, and the cause of Christianity finds every day valiant champions to devote to its service the arms which science and liberty supply. There is on the part of the Romanists a puerile infatuation upon this subject, which makes them absolutely close their eyes to facts; by an error fatal to themselves, they persist in imputing the fermentation in society, and the abandonment of religion, to the influence of the Protestant nations —nations among whom these two scourges are combated with at least as much resolution and effect as elsewhere. It is not my wish to institute disparaging comparisons, or to foment a rivalry opposed to the spirit of Christ's religion. Protestantism is not, in Christendom, the last, neither is it the sole bulwark of Christianity; but there exists none that is stronger, that offers fewer weak points to assailants, or that is better provided with faithful and able defenders.

At the commencement of this century, and in the years which followed the promulgation of the Concordat, the Protestants, like the Catholics in France, thought only of the re-establishment of their worship and of the liberty of their faith. A liberty the more precious in their eyes, as it followed upon two centuries of persecutions and of sufferings of which we cannot, in these days, read the accounts without mingled sentiments of astonishment, of indignation, and of sorrow. Faithfully should men guard the memory of such outrages; they would be infinitely better than they are if they had always present to their minds the vivid pictures of the iniquities and woes which fill the page of their history; and evils would not so soon recur if they were not so soon forgotten. The system of Terrorism under the Revolution had confounded Catholic and Protestant in a common oppression; it had abolished the forms of worship of each, denied all free expression of opinion to Christians; and without distinction condemned to the same scaffold the "pastors of the desert" and the bishops of the Court of Versailles—Rabaut Saint-Etienne as well as the nuns of Verdun. When this terrible régime had ceased to exist, neither party had religiously or politically any desires or pretensions that were not extremely moderate: the one thing regarded by all as the sovereign good was, the right to live without molestation and the liberty to address their prayers to God in the light of day. No other subject so seriously interested them; and they heartily wished to show their gratitude and deference to the Government, which, while it gave security to their bodies, permitted their souls to breathe freely. The condition of the Protestants was in one sense better than that of the Catholics, for the former were now experiencing the joy, not only of a deliverance but of a positive conquest; they had just escaped as well from the system of Terrorism, as from the ancient régime; they had lost nothing to regret; no revengeful feeling made them desire a reaction; their sole aspiration was for the consolidation of their rights, and of their new acquisitions. "You who lived, as we did, under the yoke of intolerance," (thus they were addressed in 1807 by M. Rabaut-Dupuy, formerly president of the legislative body, and the last surviving son of one of their most estimable pastors,) "you, the relics of so many persecuted generations, behold! compare! It is no longer in the desert and at the peril of your lives that you render to the Creator the homage which is his due. Our temples are restored to us, and every day beholds new ones erected. Our pastors are recognized as public functionaries; they receive salaries from the State; a barbarous law no longer suspends the sword over their heads. Alas! to those whom we have survived it was permitted, it is true, to ascend Mount Nebo, and to obtain thence a glimpse of the promised land, but it is we alone who have taken possession."

What wonder if, on the morrow after the Concordat, which had procured them the free exercise of their faith and the impartiality of the law, the Protestants acquiesced without difficulty in the incomplete organization with which the new system had left their Church, and that they troubled themselves little with the attacks made upon its independence and its dignity!

But this modest enjoyment of their new privileges did not render them indifferent to their ancient belief, and they returned to the open practice of Christ's faith simultaneously with the acquisition of their liberty. In 1812, in the midst of the profound silence which reigned throughout the Empire, a professor of the faculty of Protestant theology at Montauban, M. Gasc, attacked, in his teaching, the dogma of the Trinity. Earnest remonstrances were instantly made from the general body of the Protestants in France; a great number of consistories, among others those of Nîmes, of Montpellier, Montauban, Alais, Anduze, Saint Hippolyte, pastors and laity, addressed their complaints, some to the "Doyen" of the faculty of theology, others to M. Gasc himself, demanding, all of them, the maintenance of the doctrine of the Protestant Church. The grand master of the University, M. de Fontanes, "earnestly invited the professor not to depart from it," and M. Gasc himself admitted that his teaching ought to be in conformity. The spirit which had animated the Reformation in France in the sixteenth century was still living in the nineteenth; and under the new-born system of liberty, the Awakening of Christianity announced itself by a summons to the faith.

When, under the Restoration, France had regained her political liberty, it was not long before that liberty bore its natural fruits in French Protestantism; it was accompanied, both on religious and political subjects, by the manifestation of discordant ideas and discordant tendencies, which were soon to struggle for victory. As at epochs of great intellectual crises eminent men emerge who represent dominant ideas, so now M. Samuel Vincent and M. Daniel Encontre immediately appeared in the Protestant Church: both were pastors, and each worthily represented one of the two principles which naturally develop themselves in the bosom of Protestantism, faith in traditions and the right of private judgment; principles different without being contradictory; principles which may subsist in peace provided they remain respectively in their proper places, and within the limits of their rights. M. Samuel Vincent was a man of a mind remarkably comprehensive and of great versatility and fecundity; but his habits at the same time were those of a student, fitting him rather for intellectual meditation than qualifying him either for expansive sympathies or for action; he was versed in the philosophy and erudite criticism of Germany, at that time novel and rare to France; he made the essence of Christianity, according to his own expression, "to consist in the liberty of inquiry."* He rejected all written articles of faith, every limited idea of religious unity, and

* Vues sur le protestantisme en France, par M. Samuel Vincent. 2e édition, p. 15. Paris, 1859.

claimed within the Church, for both pastors and congregation, the greatest latitude in matters of opinion and of teaching. But when he clung closely to this view of the subject, and was pressed to indicate the extreme point to which, within the Church itself, the diversity of men's individual beliefs might be carried, his embarrassment became extreme, for he had too much sense to admit that this diversity had no limit, and that a Church, whether Protestant or not, could exist without certain articles of faith common to all its members, and recognized by them all. "Protestantism," said he himself, "must not be merely a negation; it should also have its real and positive side; it must be beyond all things a religion; that is to say, it must be in the possession of the means to endure and of the means to edify men by the propagation of a doctrine benevolent and Christian. . . . Christianity is the basis of ecclesiastical teaching." *

* Vues sur le protestantisme en France, par M. Samuel Vincent, pp. 17, 22.

When, after having laid down this principle, M. Samuel Vincent inquired how the Protestant Church could remain a Church, and a Christian Church, in the midst of the independence of individual beliefs, he found no other way out of the difficulty than "to determine," he said, "by conventions, oral and unwritten, a certain number of opinions that each man should, in the interest of the general peace, be entreated to keep to himself."* How strange a proceeding, how difficult of realization, to prescribe with once voice silence and liberty! M. Samuel Vincent did not attempt to determine what those opinions were which, in order to maintain the existence of a Christian Church in the midst of the broadest system of free inquiry, "each man should be entreated to keep to himself." As for himself, he professed his faith in the supernatural, in the revelation of the Old and of the New Testaments, in the inspiration of the Scriptures, in the divinity of Jesus Christ;

* Vues sur le protestantisme en France, p. 24.

in the grand historical facts as well as in the moral precepts of the Gospel; he was one of the pastors, too, who signed the remonstrance of the consistory of Nîmes, for the irregularity in preaching of which Professor Gasc had been guilty. Did M. Samuel Vincent regard every opinion contrary to these great evangelical doctrines as an opinion which each man should, in the interest of the general peace, be entreated to keep to himself? I doubt whether he would have dared to engraft upon the liberty of judgment such a reservation; but I doubt at the same time if he would have persisted in regarding as true and faithful pastors of the Protestant Church, men who should have openly deserted and combated, in its most essential foundations, that Christian faith which he himself professed. He dreaded almost equally "unity defined," and "dissent declared." He would have remained in the embarrassment into which those inevitably fall who neither accept one basis and manifesto of a common faith, nor admit the moral necessity of a separation into free and distinct Churches when a common faith does not exist.*

No such embarrassment was experienced by M. Daniel Encontre when he began his career to serve the movement of awakened Christianity in the bosom of French Protestantism. I will not venture here to cite the precise words, harsh and severe, employed by him on the 13th of December, 1816, at Montauban, in his capacity of "Doyen" of the faculty of Protestant Theology, respecting those termed by him "the pretended ministers of the Gospel, disbelievers in the Gospel and in the divinity of Jesus

* The principal works of M. Samuel Vincent are:

1. Vues sur le protestantisme en France, première édition. 2 vols. 8vo. 1829. A second edition, in 1 vol. 12mo., was published in 1859 by M. Prévost-Paradol.

2. Observations sur l'unité religieuse et observations sur la voie d'autorité appliquée à la religion, (1820,) contre l'Essai sur l'indifférance en matière de religion de l'Abbé de la Mennais.

3. Méditations ou recueil de sermons, 1829.

4. Mélanges de religion de morale et de critique sacrée. A periodical published from 1820 to 1825.

Christ." He regarded harmony of faith and language, harmony between shepherd and flock, as the first law of religious society. Born in a grotto of La Vaunage, to which his mother had fled to escape from the flames of persecution; devoted from his birth by his father, the Pastor Pierre Encontre, to the service of a "preacher in the desert," M. Daniel Encontre belonged to that class of indomitable Protestants who cling to their faith through all the perils, sufferings, and sacrifices which it entails. His first steps in life seemed to indicate in him other aptitudes, and to promise for him a different career. After having studied divinity at Lausanne and at Geneva, and been consecrated by his father himself to the ministry of the Gospel "in an assembly in the desert," he seemed to doubt his own vocation; for while performing the functions of his ministry he devoted himself to the study of mathematics, physics, philosophy, and the classical languages, with an enthusiasm eager to become familiar with every department of knowledge, and encountering no hinderance from internal obstacles or from preconceived opinions. Having established himself at Montpellier, where his taste for science found subjects of gratification, he led there, during the dark days of the Revolution, a life very obscure, and at the same time most laborious; giving lessons to the master masons upon stone-cutting, imparting instruction, rendering the aids of religion to Protestants, celebrating the baptismal and marriage services, and pursuing at the same time his labors in geometry, botany, philosophy, divinity, literature, and even poetry. When order began to be re-established, he was led by his own natural tastes and the counsel of his friends to select as his career that of public instruction. He competed for and obtained, first the appointment of professor of literature at the École Centrale of Montpellier; then that of the higher mathematics, at the Lycée and in the faculty of science, of which he was nominated "Doyen." As his merits established themselves by repeated proofs, his reputation increased; the papers of learned societies were filled with his contributions, and the École Polytechnique with his pupils. "I have met in our department," said Fourcroy, "two or three heads equal to his, but not one superior." M. de Candolle gladly selected him to aid him in his "Researches respecting the Botany of the Ancients;" and M. de Fontanes has more than once spoken of him to me as one of the men who most honored the University. But in him, neither the mathematician, the botanist, nor the philologist took precedence of the Christian. At one time as expounder of Moses and of Genesis,* at another as a writer defending the Apostles, accused of being a copyist of Plato,†

* Dissertation sur le vrai système du monde comparé avec le récit que Moïse fait de la création. Montpellier, 1807.

† Lettre à M. Combes-Dounous, auteur d'un Essai historique sur Platon. Paris, 1811.

A remarkable essay of M. Daniel Encontre, "sur le Péché original," was published, after his death, in 1822, and he left a great number of manuscripts, among others a "Traité sur l'Église," (600 pages,) written in Latin; "Etudes théologiques," he neglected no occasion of placing his scientific attainments at the service of Christianity; and when, in 1814, he was asked to quit Montpellier, to abandon his habits, his tastes, and his friends, for the chair of the professorship of divinity at Montauban, where he was to fulfill the functions of "Doyen," he sacrificed without hesitation the enjoyment of his life to his religious vocation, and applied himself with unceasing energy to the warlike activity of a Christian professor, until the day when, overcome by fatigue and sickness, he accorded to himself the melancholy satisfaction of returning to Montpellier, in order to die near the tomb of a beloved daughter, who had long aided him in his labors.

a Hebrew Grammar, a "Cours de philosophie," a "Cours de littérature Française," a "Flore biblique," several "Mémoires de mathématiques transcendantes," etc. As a teacher of transcendental mathematics at Montpellier he had as pupil M. Auguste Comte, the head of the "École positiviste," who, in spite of the profound diversity of their opinions, regarded it as a duty to dedicate to him in 1856 his treatise, "Sur la Synthèse subjective," in testimony of admiration and of gratitude.

The destinies of Protestantism in France have, to a singular degree, been at once varied and uniform, confused and simple. After having in the sixteenth century valiantly disputed the victory, it was vanquished, decimated, expelled. But it resisted, and survived not only its defeat, but the gradual process of its enfeeblement and its expulsion. In the course of the seventeenth and eighteenth centuries the French Protestants lost the protection of the laws, their secure sanctuaries, their great chiefs, their great divines, their great writers; but they preserved nevertheless their faith and their religious honor. In the times that ensued their successors remained faithful to the belief and the customs of their fathers; even persecuted and condemned to death, having their property confiscated, or become tenants of prisons and laborers in the galleys, they found in their very sufferings a resource to confirm them in the principles of Protestant piety. Theological controversies died away from among them, leaving behind them the fundamentals of Christianity—living and guiding principles.

Among the higher and wealthier classes, the philosophical ideas of the eighteenth century made also their way; the great liberal movement filled the Protestant section of the nation with joy, and commanded its sympathy without detaching it from its religious habits and traditions. In its members faith had ceased to be erudite; the popular Protestant sentiment had been always profoundly biblical and evangelical. Freer and more fortunately situated than their fathers, the French Protestants now anxiously desired to remain, as they had been, Christians; and when, in 1790, Rabaut Saint-Etienne, who succeeded the Abbé de Montesquieu as President of the Constituent Assembly, wrote to his aged father, the Pastor Paul Rabaut, "The President of the National Assembly is at your feet," he manifested to the humble and zealous preacher in the assemblies of the desert, the pride at once of a politician, the piety of a son, and the fidelity of a Protestant.

M. Daniel Encontre was, at the commencement of the nineteenth century, the faithful representative of this traditionally religious character of French Protestantism; just as M. Samuel Vincent was the well-meaning and sincere introducer to it of the science and criticism of the Germans. The former corresponded more closely to the pious and national spirit of Protestant France of the olden times; the latter to the tendencies, at once novel and indefinitely latitudinarian, of a foreign philosophy and a foreign erudition. Doubtless, neither measured the range of the religious crisis of which they were themselves the symptoms; neither foresaw that within the bosom of Protestantism that crisis was to be marked by an avowed struggle between Rationalism in its progress and Christianity in its reaction.

This crisis began to manifest itself at Geneva.

The mocking skepticism of Voltaire, the rhetorical deism of Rousseau, proclaimed at its gates, had deeply undermined the faith of Christ in the very city of Calvin. It was not merely some of the Calvinistic doctrines of the sixteenth century that the pastors of Geneva doubted or denied, but it was also the fundamental articles of Christianity; they abandoned not only the dogmas of predestination and salvation by faith alone, but the dogmas of original sin, and of the divinity of Jesus Christ. In 1810 according to some, as far back as 1802 according to others, symptoms of an evangelical reaction showed themselves at Geneva among the students in theology, some of whom afterward became distinguished pastors or writers. It was not long before MM. Gaussen, Malan, Gonthier, Bost, Merle d'Aubigné, displayed their orthodox fervor and their ability. In 1816 a pious Scot, Mr. Robert Haldane, previously an intrepid sailor, who had only quitted his calling to devote himself entirely to the service of his faith, went to Geneva, and contracted with the young Methodists of that city relations of the greatest intimacy and activity. They had meetings; they discussed, they preached, they prayed, they wrote. Mr. Haldane could hardly express himself in French; having his English Bible continually at hand, he turned over its pages incessantly, pointed out to his friends the passages that he regarded as decisive, invited them to read them aloud from their French Bible, and then commented upon them in a manner that always commanded their favorable attention, the conviction of the commentator had such moving and persuasive power.*

In 1816 and 1817 the evangelical reaction made rapid progress, and the body of Genevese pastors resolved to combat it by the voice of authority. They found, however, no better method of doing so than by insisting upon

* Genève religieuse au XIX siècle: par le Baron de Goltz; traduit de l'allemand par C. Malan: 8vo., pp. 137–149. Genève et Paris. 1862.

what, twelve years later, even M. Samuel Vincent did not scruple to recommend; they prescribed silence even whilst they proclaimed liberty. "Without"—these are their words—"giving any judgment upon the questions really involved, and without controlling in any respect the liberty of opinions," they imposed a solemn engagement both upon students demanding to be consecrated to the sacred ministry, and upon ministers candidates for pastoral functions in the Church of Geneva. It was conceived as follows: "As long as we reside and preach in the churches of the Canton of Geneva, we promise to abstain from establishing, either in entire discourses or in parts of discourses directed to this object, our opinion—first, of the manner in which the divine nature was incarnate in the person of Jesus Christ; secondly, of original sin; thirdly, of the mode in which grace operates, or grace is efficient; fourthly, of predestination. We promise also not to combat, in any public discourse, the opinion of any pastors or ministers touching these subjects."*

It is difficult to understand how men ever could have flattered themselves with the hope of re-establishing peace in the Church by the employment of so sorry an expedient. Liberty, that has rent asunder such heavy chains, does not permit itself to be confined by so flimsy a net. The immediate effect of the regulation of the Genevese pastors was an outburst of discontent. The more violent Methodists, MM. Malan and Bost at their head, proclaimed aloud their separation from the established Church; the more moderate, among others, MM. Gaussen and Merle d'Aubigné, persisted in remaining, by right of their ministry, in its bosom, holding themselves responsible representatives *there* of the doctrines of the Reformation, which, in fact, they did continue to preach and to teach. The body of pastors at first used great for-

* Genève religieuse au XIX siècle: par le Baron de Goltz; p. 153.

bearance toward them, and respected their liberty; and when the populace, irritated at the agitation caused in families by the Dissenters, and offended by the austerity of their precepts, made hostile demonstrations toward them, the Council of Geneva had the wisdom and fairness to use measures of repression; but, soon becoming weary of this painful duty, the Council formally forbade, without its express permission, any book of religious controversy to be printed at Geneva. The body of pastors soon pronounced as vehement a condemnation of the moderate Methodists as of the ultra Dissenters. The moderate Methodists then in their turn resorted to energetic measures in support of their cause: they founded an evangelical society and a school of theology; devoted the one to propagate the zeal and the other to teach the principles of the Christian reaction; and fifteen years after the commencement of the struggle, the chiefs of the party which had proclaimed that the free divergence of individual belief in the bosom of the Church was "the great fact of our epoch, and the great step that the Reformation had in our days to make"—these chiefs, being the body of pastors, the Consistory, and the Council of State at Geneva, suspended M. Gaussen from his functions of pastor in the parish of Satigny for having taken part in the organization of an independent form of worship, and of a school of independent theology; "a proceeding," they said, "incompatible with the peace of the Church, and to be regarded as an act of insubordination, tending to bring ecclesiastical authority into discredit."*

Such religious ferment in the primitive home of the French Reformation, and at the very gates of France, could not fail to exercise a powerful influence upon the French Protestant Church. On quitting Geneva in 1817, Mr. Robert Haldane proceeded to Montauban, where he formed friendships with some of the

* Genève religieuse au XIX siècle: par le Baron de Goltz; pp. 379–384.

Professors of the Faculty, and among others with M. Daniel Encontre. He published there also a work in French, which his friends hastened to circulate. It was styled "Emmanuel: vues Scripturaires sur Jésus-Christ." In 1818, a society formed in England, named the "Continental Society," specially devoted itself to the purpose of seconding on the Continent the progress of this Christian reaction. An English dissenter, Mr. Mark Wilks, pastor of the American community formed at Paris, was the most efficient agent of the societies which had this object in view. "It might be said of Mr. Wilks," wrote lately the Pastor Juillerat, "that he might have governed an empire, his character was so energetic, his mind so active and enterprising. He brought me aid of every description: money was required, he had money; pamphlets and books were wanted, no one was better provided; no one understood better the details pertaining to the printing and publication of papers." Several Protestant journals and magazines, "La Voix de la Religion Chrétienne au XIX siècle," "Les Archives du Christianisme au XIX siècle," "Les Mélanges de Religion, de Morale, et de Critique Sacrée," "L'Evangeliste," "La Revue Protestante," "Le Semeur," etc., etc., were at this epoch successively founded and carried in different directions throughout the scattered Protestant Church, from its central organization, the fervor which had there been kindled. Genuine zeal for religion is not satisfied by action from a distance, or by action upon unknown persons, or by indirect means, as by books and by journals: it demands direct oral communication from man to man—the union of men's souls in common prayer. Certain young pastors who had at first shared in the evangelical movement at Geneva, MM. Neff, Pyt, Bost, Gonthier, scattered themselves over France, some assuming functions as local pastors, others as traveling missionaries, attracting to their proximity groups of zealous Protestants, animating the lukewarm, and erecting in every place where they made any stay little centers of Christianity, which radiated to the neighboring country around. Distinct associations, some officially recognized by the State, others having no public character,* gave to the labors of isolated individuals the publicity, the unity, the permanence which they required; and a special organization (colportage biblique) which at its commencement numbered only seven, but a few years afterward had sixty agents, all of them, although obscure individuals, as zealous as their patrons were zealous, caused the Holy Scriptures and religious tracts to penetrate into parts of France hopelessly inaccessible to any other method of communication and of instruction.

To a movement so earnest and so general, although propagated by a small number of per-

* La Société biblique, la Société pour l'encouragement de l'instruction primaire parmi les protestants, la Société évangélique de France, la Société des traités religieuse, la Société des missions protestantes, la Société centrale pour les intérêts protestants, la Société d'évangelisation, etc.

sons in the heart of a population itself forming but a small minority in the nation at large, obstacles would inevitably occur. They were encountered on all hands and of all kinds, religious and political—from the administration, from popular prejudices, from the distrust of the Government, from the hostility of the Roman Catholic clergy, from differences of opinion on theological points among Protestants themselves, from the *amour propre* of individuals, and the perplexed or timorous ideas of subalterns in authority. The activity of the Protestant societies created uneasiness in bishops and priests, who strove not merely to counteract their influence, but to interfere with their liberty of action. Mayors of towns, judges of the peace, sometimes too, magistrates and administrators of more elevated rank, lent their aid to these exceptionable proceedings. Hence arose suspicions, complaints, and struggles which retarded the new-born impulse of awakening Christianity. But the earnest perseverance of its patrons, the general wisdom of the supreme Government, and the authority, growing more and more each day, of the principles of justice and of liberty, gradually surmounted all these obstacles. It was the Restoration that recognized the chief Protestant societies and gave them the sanction of the law. Under the Government of 1830 they used their rights with more confidence and fewer hinderances. The equitable intentions of King Louis Philippe and of his counselors upon religious matters could not be doubtful, whatever their caution not to cause uneasiness or wound the susceptibilities of the Roman Catholics. The Protestants now believed it to be no longer necessary to look to foreign support. Formed at Paris in 1833, the Evangelical Society of France experienced a momentary impulse of national jealousy, the result of which was some coldness in its relations with the Continental Society of London; but as soon as the latter perceived that its direct interference was rather an embarrassment than a necessity to the Christian reaction in France, it withdrew its agency without withholding its sympathy, and handed over to the Evangelical Society of France all the "stations" and religious charities which had up to that time been founded by its exertions.

The awakening of Christianity among the Protestants of France had now produced such results that it mattered little who the patrons of the movement might be; it had assumed its true character, and was drawing its strength from the fountain of truth. In times of religious incredulity and of religious indifference, and even in the transitional times which immediately ensue, it is the error of many, and even of men who respect and support religion, to consider it in the light of a great political institution—a salutary system of moral police, however necessary to society, indebted for its merits and its prerogatives rather to its practical utility than to its intrinsic truth. Grave error, misconceiving both the nature and the origin of religion, and calculated to deprive it both of its empire and its dignity! Utility men hold as of great account, but it is only truth that commands unconditional surrender. Utility enjoins prudence and forbearance; truth alone inspires feelings of confidingness and devotion. A religion having no other guarantee for its influence and its endurance than its social utility would be very near its ruin. Men have need of, nay, they thirst for truth in their relations with God, even more than in their relations with one another; the spontaneous prayer, adoration, obedience, suppose faith. It was in the very name of the verity of the Christian religion, of that verity manifested in its history by the word and even by the presence of God, that the awakening of Christians was accomplished among us. The laborers in this great work felt the faith of Christianity, and they diffused it; had they spoken only of the social utility of Christianity, they would never have made the conquest of a single human soul.

At first sight one is tempted to attribute this success to energy of faith on the part of these laborers in the cause, to the active and devoted perseverance of their zeal. Again a mistake! Not that human merit was without its share in the results; but even where the faith was thus propagated, the share that that faith itself had in the result was infinitely greater, from its own proper and inherent virtue, than any share of men. Incredulity and indifferentism may diffuse themselves and pretend to dominate; they leave unsolved the problems that lie in the depth of man's soul: they do not rid him of his perplexities, of instinct or of reflection, as to the world's creation and man's creation, the origin of good and evil, providence and fate, human liberty and human responsibility, man's immortality and his future state. Instead of the denials and the doubts that had been thrown over these unescapable questions, those who applied themselves fully to rouse awakened Christianity, recalled the human soul to the memory of positive solutions of these questions; solutions in accordance with the traditions of their native land, in accordance with their habits as members of families, and in harmony with the recollections of early childhood; solutions often contested, never refuted; always recurring in the lapse of ages, and century after century! It was from the intrinsic and permanent value of the doctrines which they were preaching, and not from themselves, that the laborers in the work derived their force and their credit.

They had another principle of force as well; a force born and developed in the bosom of the Christian religion, and in that alone; they had the passionate desire to save human souls. Men are not, they never have been, struck as they ought to have been struck with the beauty of this passion, or with its novelty in the moral history of the world, or with the part that it has played among Christian nations. Before the era of Christianity, in times of Asiatic and

European antiquity, pagans and philosophers busied themselves about the destiny of men after the close of their earthly life, and with curiosity, too, did they sound the obscurity; but the ardent solicitude for the eternal welfare of human souls, the never-wearying labor to prepare human souls for eternity—to set them even during this existence in intimate relations with God, and to prepare them to undergo God's judgments;—we have in all this a fact essentially Christian, one of the sublimest characteristics of Christianity, and one of the most striking marks of its divine origin. God constantly in relation with mankind and with every man, God present during the actual life of every man, and God the arbiter of his future destiny; the immortality of each human soul, and the connection between his actual life and his future destiny; the immense value of each human soul in the eyes of God, and the immense import to the soul of the future that awaits it: these are the convictions and the affirmations all implied in the one passion alluded to, the passion for the salvation of men's souls, which was the whole life of our Saviour Jesus Christ, which passed by his example and by his precepts into the life of his primitive disciples, and which, amid the diversities of age, people, manners, opinions, has remained the characteristic feature and the inspiring breath of the genius of Christianity; breath which animated the men who in our days labored, and with success, to revive Christian faith among the Protestants of France!

Their zeal was employed in a very circumscribed sphere; beyond it their names were unknown, and unknown they have remained. What spectators, what readers, what public knew at that time, or know even at this moment, what manner of men they were or what their deeds—those men who called themselves Neff, Bost, Pyt, Gonthier, Audebez, Cook, Wilks, Haldane? But who, I would ask, in the time of Tacitus and of Pliny, knew what manner of men they were, and what the deeds of Peter, Paul, John, Matthew, Philip—the unknown disciples of the Master, unknown himself, who had overcome the world? Notoriety is not essential to influence; and in the sphere of the soul, as in the order of nature, fountains are not the less abundant because their springs are hidden in obscurity. The Christian missionaries of our time did not trouble themselves to lessen that obscurity. To literary celebrity they had no pretension, nor did they seek the triumph of any political idea, of any specific system of ecclesiastical organization, of any favorite plan in which their personal vanity was interested: the salvation of human souls was their only passion, and their only object. They looked upon themselves as humble servants commissioned to remind men of promises which they had forgotten—of promises of salvation by faith in Jesus. "The stir of the reaction," one of themselves has said, "bore impressed upon it the character of youth, or even of childhood. The humblest pastor on his circuit became a missionary; his transit was regarded almost like that of a meteor. On the instant an assembly was convoked, it numbered twenty, thirty, fifty, a hundred, two hundred persons, collected to listen joyfully, as if it were a great novelty or miracle, to that Gospel which we know by heart;—alas! which we know by heart far more than we have it in the heart!"*

Who could mistake, on hearing such sentiments and such language, the really Christian character of the reaction?

Never-ending weakness of man's nature, and inevitable imperfection of man's work, even when man is walking in the ways of God! In the midst of awakening Christianity, and of this fervent return to the faith of the Gospel, reappeared some of the ancient pretensions of theology, and among others the pretension to

*Mémoires pouvant servir à l'histoire du réveil religieux des églises protestantes de la Suisse et de la France, par A. Bost, (1854,) t. 1, p. 240.

penetrate the decrees of God and to define the terms of man's salvation.

In February, 1818, the pious and orthodox "Doyen" of the Protestant Faculty of Montauban, M. Daniel Encontre, rendering an account of the work of Mr. Robert Haldane, (Emmanuel, ou vues Scripturaires sur Jésus-Christ,) which had just appeared, hastened, after having justly commended it, to add: "The concluding pages of the 'Emmanuel' express sentiments which Evangelical Christians are far from sharing. The author lays down the principle, that all men who do not believe in the perfect equality of the *Son* and of the *Father*, are enemies alike of both *Father* and *Son;* that they deny, and blaspheme against both, and cannot avoid eternal death. He regards the forbearance we show to them as infinitely criminal, and seems even inclined to condemn all who have not the courage to condemn them. As for me, I venture to believe that it is the duty of a Christian to work out his own salvation without allowing himself to pronounce upon the salvation of others. *Judge not, that ye be not judged*, says He whom we all acknowledge as our Master; and St. Paul adds, '*Who art thou* that condemnest another man's servant?' I seize this opportunity to declare to all men desirous to hear it, that I believe firmly in the divinity of our Lord Jesus Christ, and that I adopt in every respect the Nicæan Creed. I dare to affirm besides, that these sentiments are actually those of all the members of our Faculty, as they have always been those of our Churches. It seems to me that persons who know not Jesus Christ as 'God above all things, blessed eternally,' are much to be pitied, and want the greatest of all consolations. This error appears the more dangerous, because it is generally followed by other errors; for the truths which are the objects of faith are so connected and riveted together, that it is impossible to discard one without shaking or overturning all the others. These truths form together a majestic edifice, to which all its parts are absolutely necessary, and which falls in ruins if a breach be made anywhere; and particularly, if the first stone removed be the keystone of the corner. But what would become of us all, if the erring, even when they err in good faith, had no hope of access to the throne of grace? Men who, as I do, feel how much they need God's mercy, and man's indulgence, feel little disposition to be severe toward others."*

In holding this language, M. Encontre was not merely performing, on his own account, an act of humility and of Christian charity; he was touching upon one of the supreme questions which, in our days, are occasioning a crisis in Christendom; and he was indicating its true and its sole solution. Like all passions, (the best are not exempt,) the passion for the salvation of man's soul is full of enthusiasm and full of blindness; it believes too readily in the possibility of attaining the object; it is too unscrupulous and undiscriminating in the means.

* Archives du Christianisme aux XIXe siècle, t. 1, pp. 63–66.

Hence sprung religious tyranny and theological intolerance: the powerful thought they could compel the human soul to work out its own salvation; the learned believed they could define the conditions of that salvation. Mistakes, both of them, profoundly antichristian! Just as no power of man has the right to strip any single soul, created by God free and responsible, of its liberty of conscience; so, equally, no science of man can define the laws and the facts that shall regulate the future state of the soul. Liberty is, on this earth, the principle of the moral life of man; man's state beyond this earth is a question between him and his Maker, and to be determined by the use which man may have here made of his liberty. To respect God's gift of liberty to man, and the mystery of God's decrees respecting man's salvation, is in reality the law of Christians; and it is only on this double condition that there really is either any awakening or any progress of Christians.

Nothing does more honor to the memory of

M. Daniel Encontre than to have been one of the first to understand and to fulfill this double duty. Firmly attached to those fundamental articles of belief which are Christianity itself, he was strange to every narrowness or exaggeration of doctrine, to every presumptuousness of opinion, and to every theological intolerance; his piety was comprehensive, without there being any vagueness in his faith; his Christianity was that of a Liberal; nor did his attainments as a mathematician indispose him to remain a Christian.

Scarcely was M. Encontre dead, when two new men, both, like him, eminent as pastors and professors—M. Alexandre Vinet and M. Adolphe Monod—appeared on the religious arena, and gave more éclat to the Christian reaction by using similar means, and by impelling the Protestant Church of France in the same direction.

Although he was born and continually lived and wrote in Switzerland, M. Alexandre

Vinet was of French extraction; he belongs to France as much as to Switzerland, for he knew, and understood, and loved France as much as he did Switzerland. He served, too, the cause of religious liberty, and the Christian reaction, in France not less than in Switzerland. A delicate child, son of a poor and an austere schoolmaster, who destined him to the obscure life of a village clergyman, he manifested from the commencement of his laborious career an ardent taste for literature and for study, which promised him a rich reward in the intellectual enjoyment of the chef-d'œuvres of ancient and modern literature. He was found upon one occasion in his little chamber in a fit of enthusiasm and affected to tears by a perusal of the "Cid." At the age of twenty he became Professor of French Literature at Bâle; and there he devoted himself to the service of every candidate upon the Rhine or upon the Swiss Alps who required to be taught to comprehend and admire the great writers of France of whatever age, and in whatever department of literature. Philosophers and orators, prose-writers and poets, Christians or Freethinkers, Catholics or Protestants, Conservatives or Reformers, Classicists or Romanticists—all the men who have constituted the intellectual and literary glory of France, obtained in this fervent Methodist of the Valdenses an admirer as warm as he was intelligent and impartial. The prevailing characteristic of M. Vinet's literary essays and criticisms is their geniality; and wherever he encounters any spark or trace of the true or the beautiful, under whatever banner they appear, and however they may be mingled with opinions otherwise shocking to his feelings, he is at once attracted and moved, and he admires and praises with enthusiasm. His was a mind of comprehensive sympathies, open to every impression, keen to appreciate, always ready to enjoy everything that deserved to give pleasure, even although it might be only momentarily and in passing.

This passionate admirer of the beautiful, this critic, so liberal-minded and so impartial, was a sound and uncompromising moralist, as well as a pious and firm Christian. The predominant idea of all his literary judgments is moral; and this determines the tone of his criticism, and the impression which it leaves behind it, without ever rendering it either harsh, or illiberal, or narrow-minded. In the sphere of positive belief, without importing into controversies between believer and believer any microscopic criticism of detail, M. Vinet has never, upon the divine origin and the fundamental dogmas of Christianity, had the least hesitation, never made the smallest concession; he grapples directly with the most specious and the most popular objections of his adversaries, and combats them with a conviction the expression of which becomes more and more eloquent the clearer and the more complete its manifestation. "To attempt to distinguish morality from dogma," he says, "is to attempt to distinguish a river from its source. The Christian dogma is at its outset a morality, although a Christian one. Just as God, in the creed of Christianity, reveals himself under a form that nature did not announce, Christian morality, in its turn, invests itself with a character that nature would never have impressed upon it. Man finding his own inability to make himself a religion, God came to aid him in his weakness. It is now rather more than eighteen centuries since, in an obscure corner of the world, there appeared a man. I do not say that a long series of prophets had announced the coming of that man; that a long series of miracles had marked with the seal of God the nation where he was to be born, and even the prophecy which foretold him; that, in a word, an imposing mass of evidence surrounds and authenticates him. I say merely that that man preached a religion. That religion is not natural religion; the dogmas of the existence of God and of the soul's immortality are everywhere taken for granted in his discourses—never taught, never proved. Neither are the ideas which he teaches deduced logically from the primitive axioms of reason; that which he teaches, that which forms the substance of his doctrine, embraces subjects which confound the reason, and to which the reason has neither way nor access; he preaches a God on earth, a God man, a God poor, a God crucified; he preaches wrath involving the innocent, mercy exempting the guilty from all condemnation, God the victim of man, and man forming one person with God; he preaches a new birth, without which man can never be saved; he preaches the sovereignty of God's grace, and the plenitude of the liberty of man. I do not in any way qualify his teaching; I give them to you as they are, and without disguise; I seek not to justify them. You may, if you please, feel surprise, you may take offense; scruple not to do so. But when you have to your heart's content wondered at their strangeness, I on my side will propose to you another subject for your wonder. These strange dogmas conquered the world. In their very infancy they invaded learned Athens, rich Corinth, haughty Rome. They gathered together 'Confessors' from workshops, from prisons, from schools, from the courts of justice, and from thrones. Conquerors of civilization, they triumphed over barbarism; they made to pass under the same yoke the degraded Roman, the savage Sicambrian. The forms of society have changed; society has been dissolved and moulded afresh. They alone have endured in their integrity. No other doctrine, whether of philosophy or of religion, lasted: each had its time; each time its idea; and, as a celebrated writer has said, the religious sentiment, abandoned to itself, chose for itself moulds in accordance with the time, which it broke when the time was no longer there. But the dogma of the Cross persisted in recurring. Had it only taken possession of a certain class of persons it would have been much, it would perhaps have been even inexplicable; but you find followers of the Cross in the camp and in civil life, among the rich and among the poor, among the bold and among the timid, among the learned and among the ignorant. This dogma is good for all, everywhere, always; it never grows old. The religion of the Cross appears nowhere in arrear of civilization; on the contrary, far as civilization may progress, it ever finds Christianity in advance. Suppose not that a complaisant Christianity will ever cancel any article or expunge any idea to accommodate itself to the age: no, it derives its strength from its inflexibility, and needs not make any surrender to be in harmony with what is beautiful, legitimate, true; for it is in itself the type of them all. Still it is not a religion which flatters man; and the worldly, by keeping aloof, show plainly enough that Christianity is a strange doctrine. Those who dare not reject it strive to render it palatable. They strip it of what offends them—of its myths, as they are pleased to style them; they almost make out of Christ's doctrine a *rationalism.* But, singular to say, once a rationalism it has no longer any force; in this respect resembling one of the most marvelous creatures in the animate world, to which it is death to lose its sting. The *strange* dogmas disappear, but with them all zeal, fervor, sanctity, charity, disappear also; the salt of the earth has lost its savor, and we know not by what means to restore it. But, on the other hand, do you learn that somewhere or other there is an awakening of Christians, that Christianity is resuscitating, that faith shows signs of life, that zeal abounds? Ask not in what soil these precious plants are springing; you may pronounce yourself: it is in the rude and rugged soil of orthodoxy, in the shade of the mysteries which confound human reason, and of which human reason would like so much to get rid. . . . Some passages in the fair work of M. Saint-Marc Girardin upon dramatic literature might, at least I fear so, lead to the conclusion that Christianity is, in its essence, only the result of a natural progress of man's mind, a gradual development of ancient wisdom. Such, for instance, is the passage where the author tells us that the Greeks were advancing step by step toward Christian spiritualism. We regret that M. Saint-Marc Girardin did not say in what sense he understood this, and within what limits. We hope that he will not see in us the champion of a captious orthodoxy, if we say that nothing so much weakens the authority of Christianity, that nothing prejudices in men's minds its cause more, than to treat it as a link in the chain, which chain in reality it severed. That events, that is, Providence, did aforehand hollow a bed in the regions of the west for this divine river, what believer, however rigid, would ever entertain any scruple in admitting? But still it is essential that we should not misapprehend the source whence that river welled forth. No natural development of events, either among the Jews or among the Greeks, can account for the existence of Christianity. Whatever the progress made by the ancients, there never was a time when there existed not an infinity between their ideas, and the ideas of Christianity; and infinity alone can fill up the gulf between. There is an end of Christianity if men agree in thinking the contrary—if they succeed in causing the Supernatural to assume a place in one of the compartments of the Philosophy of History. As far as we are concerned, we would prefer for the Christian religion the most outrageous denial, to an admiration circumscribed within such limits. Christ's faith is nothing if not, like Melchisedek without earthly parent here below, and without genealogy." *

Whoever indicated with greater distinctness the keystone in the edifice of Christianity, or ever clung to it more closely? M. Vinet occu-

* Essai sur la manifestation des convictions religieuses, p. 85. Premiers discours, pp. 14, 50, 53. Littérature Française, vol. iii, p. 623.

pied himself in turn with freedom of conscience and of man's thought, with the faith of Christ, and with the literature of France. These three subjects became the passions of his life, stirring his soul, though at unequal depths. But of these three only one, the passion for literature, was a source to him of tranquil and unmitigated enjoyment. In his advocacy of man's liberty and of Christianity, M. Vinet had to pass not only through the ordeal of intellectual labors and combats, but through the solicitudes and sorrows of life. The defender of the liberty of forms of worship, crowned as such by the "Société Français de la Morale Chrétienne," lived to see this liberty attacked in his native Switzerland, at once by popular fury and by civil authority. The fervent promoter of the Christian reaction beheld one hundred and sixty evangelical pastors of the Canton of the Vaud, his companions in this pious work, forced to quit their "Chairs" in order to preserve their faith. And it was in sickness, and at the approach of death, that M. Vinet had to undergo all this. Neither his faith nor the tranquillity of his soul was disturbed. He continued, to his last hour, to be the active champion of liberty, the faithful servant of Christ, the eloquent admirer and commentator upon French literature, which he followed in all its phases, whether calm or stormy, whether pure or defiled. "After all," so he wrote in 1845, "I am not one of those who despair; God, without any violence to our freedom of action, rather by that freedom itself, conducts us to the unknown shores. The ports at which we land do not all of them afford secure mooring; we know something of that even in this little country. Our progress will be slow, and amid storms; but the circle of universal truth will be completed, and man's sense of moral right and wrong will be improved, at the same time that man's science will be enriched. I should feel horror if I thought that *Some One* is not at the center of all this movement, holding all its elements in his hand; *Some*

One to whom, whether they know him or do not know him, the aspirations of all creatures ascend in their sorrow, and whom they instinctively salute with the sweet reassuring name of 'Father.'"*

Upon a single point, the relations of Church and State, his usual comprehensiveness of view and independence of thought appeared to abandon M. Vinet. Justly struck and afflicted by his own experience of the inconveniences of a strict bond between Church and State, dis-

*Notice sur M. Alexandre Vinet, par M. E. Souvestre, published in the Magazin Pittoresque de 1848, p. 81.

The principal works of M. Alexandre Vinet are:

1. Traité et Polémique sur la liberté des cultes. 1826, 1852.
2. Discours sur quelques sujets religieux. 1831, 1853.
3. Essais de philosophie et de morale religieuse. 1837.
4. Essai sur la manifestation des convictions religieuses, et sur la séparation de l'Église et de État. 1842, 1858.
5. Études et méditations évangéliques. 1847, 1849, 1851.
6. Études sur Pascal. 1848, 1856.
7. Chrestomathie Française, Histoire de la littérature Française au XVIII siècle, et Études sur la littérature Française au XIXe siècle. 1829, 1849, 1853, etc.

He wrote, besides, numerous short pieces, and articles in reviews and journals, suggested by topics of the day.

gusted at the servility and falsity which frequently are, sometimes on the part of the State, sometimes on the part of the Church, its results, he concluded that in all cases all alliance between the two conditions of society is radically vicious; and he declared their entire separation a general and absolute principle, the sole reasonable and just system, the sole efficacious guarantee of truth and of liberty in spirituals or temporals. He thus ignored, it appears to me, the natural causes which produce, and the human motives which sanction, a certain alliance between societies civil and ecclesiastical; he ignored also the inestimable advantages which, at certain times and in certain circumstances, each may derive, and has actually derived, from that alliance. In the United States of America, the entire separation of the State and of the different Churches was necessary and salutary, for it was the spontaneous consequence of the condition of men's minds, and of the position of society. In England, in spite of the acts of injustice, and the ills engendered by the intimate union of the state with a Church legally constituted and having exclusive privileges, the coexistence of the Church of England with the freedom, more and more every day complete and recognized, of the Churches of the Dissenters, was for the Christian religion a potent principle of life, of force, and of durability.

And if we go back to the ancient history of Europe, who can doubt that at the fall of the Roman Empire, if the State and the Church had not, although distinct institutions, been allied, the development of Christianity would have been far less energetic, and its conquest of its barbarous conquerors far more problematical? This is, I repeat, a question not of principle, but of time, of place, of circumstance, and of condition of society. A complete separation of Church and State may be good and practicable; it is neither the only good system, nor is it always a practicable system.

An alliance of the two upon certain fixed

terms has its inconveniences and its perils, but its effects may be also very salutary; it may be essential, and does not of necessity exclude religious sincerity or religious liberty. M. Vinet, in discussing the subject, lost sight of the general history of human societies, and attached too much importance to the specious and transient facts which he had before his eyes.

If M. Vinet were now living, he might in his own country behold two fair examples of the good results of the mixed systems which he so absolutely condemned. In the Cantons of the Vaud and of Geneva, after the violent and painful contests to which I have above referred, a dissenting Independent Church was established by the side of a Church recognized and supported by the State. In neither canton was this establishment a temporary expedient, the fruit of a momentary ardor; the Independent Church has consolidated and developed itself; it endures and prospers. Like the Establishment, it has its pastors, its churches, its solemnities, its schools for general and for superior instruction. I have before me facts and figures which prove its vitality and its progress. And not only did the Established Church finally acquiesce in the peaceable existence of the Independent Church, it also profited by it, and its salutary influence has been frankly acknowledged by its worthiest pastors. In Switzerland, as in England, Scotland, and Holland, and in our days more easily and more promptly than in ancient times, the existence on the one side of a national Church recognized by the State, has given to the different forms of Christian belief a stability and a dignity which have secured its permanent effects upon succeeding generations; the existence, on the other side, of independent Churches, and the religious emulation between the two establishments, have turned in both to the profit of faith and of piety.

M. Adolphe Monod seemed, even more than M. Vinet, to promise by natural bent of his character, and by the incidents of his life, to become the champion of an entire separation of Church and State. At the very commencement of his career, he suffered from a Government based upon their connection. Pastor at Lyons, in 1831, of the established Protestant Church, he was dismissed from these functions by the Consistory of that city, as too exacting in his orthodoxy, and as troubling by his exigencies the peace of his Church. He then became the founder and pastor of a small dissenting and independent Church at Lyons. The energy with which he expressed his convictions, and the excellence of his preaching, rapidly spread, and increased his renown for piety. Numerous Protestants manifested the desire to see him once more within the pale of the national Church. He made no objection; a Chair becoming vacant in the Faculty of Montauban, M. Adolphe Monod was nominated, and from 1836 to 1847 he both lectured and preached at Montauban with a commanding ability that made itself felt, not only among the majority of the students, but propagated its influences to a distance among the principal centers of French Protestantism. In 1847 he was summoned to Paris as the suffragan of another pastor, M. Juillerat. Nor did he scruple to accept this secondary and precarious situation. He had full confidence in the divine vocation, and was firmly resolved to proceed to any place where the faith of Christ might demand his services. He had, in the evangelical chair, even more success at Paris than at Lyons and Montauban. When, after the Revolution of 1848, a general assembly of the Reformed Churches of France assembled for the purposes of considering their institutions and discussing points of common interest, a grave question was raised, and became the subject of warm and lengthened debate: Should French Protestants proclaim their ancient Confession of Faith, that of Rochelle, or should they proclaim a confession of new articles; or lastly, should they remain passive and do nothing? some, and particularly their pastor, M. Frederic Monod, elder brother of M. Adolphe Monod, announced their determination to retire from the assembly and from the established Church, unless they adopted a Confession of Faith in accordance with the traditional principles of the Reformation. The inertness of the hesitating and timid assembly was equivalant to a refusal, and they did in effect retire. To the great surprise and great regret of his adversaries, M. Adolphe Monod, although favorable to the principles of the Confession of Faith, did not follow the example by retiring; he even succeeded his brother as titular pastor in the Church of Paris, and published to the world the motives of his conduct.*

His motives were good, such as a man of elevated character and energetic purpose might conceive and might avow. In spite of their importance, the questions which concern the

* In his work entitled, Pourquoi je demeure dans l'Église établie.

organization of the Church and its eternal relations were, in the eyes of M. Adolphe Monod, only secondary considerations, subject in a certain measure to time and to circumstance. For him the question of faith was supreme; and he occupied himself infinitely more with the spiritual state of souls than with ecclesiastical government. To the serious thinker the Christian faith is quite different from any conception or conviction of the understanding; it is a general condition of the whole man; it is the very life of the soul; not merely its actual life, but the source and the guarantee of its future life. The faith in Christ Jesus, the Redeemer, the Saviour, makes the life of a Christian; and the life of a Christian is a preparation for an eternal salvation. With this faith penetrating to his very marrow, and with the intimate persuasion of its consequences, the duty of giving a voice to that faith, and of diffusing it, was the dominant idea, the permanent passion, of M. Adolphe Monod. He had not himself been always firmly settled in his religious convictions; he had been a prey to great moral perplexities, and to attacks of profound melancholy. When he had escaped from these—or rather, to use his own words, "when God had become really the master of his heart"—he had no other thought but that of bringing other souls to the same state, and of rousing them to a faith in Christ, with a view to their eternal salvation. The position which he regarded as of all the most appropriate for himself, was one in which he could most profitably forward this work. When in 1848 the question was thus put to him, and when he had been convinced both by his past observation of the Protestant Church of France during the last twenty years, and by his own experience of it, that the established Church offered to him in his Christian purpose the vastest field of exertion, and the best chance of success, he did not hesitate to remain in it. "I find in the situation," he said, "grave disorders, of which it is my duty to seek unceasingly the reform; but that situation has also its hopeful side. A long development of my ideas would be superfluous; let us confine ourselves to some striking facts. Try and reckon how many orthodox pastors our Church possessed when the reaction began in 1819, and then make a similar calculation for 1849. I do not mean to fix the precise numbers; but is it too much to say, that in the course of a single generation the number of orthodox pastors is ten, fifteen, twenty times perhaps as great? This applies to the clergy, of whom everywhere the immense influence is felt. Among their congregations it is less easy to follows things; but the attentive observer does not fail to mark similar indications. Behold our religious societies: are not the most popular among them those which hoisted most manfully the colors of orthodoxy? And if some are in a languishing condition, is it not because they offered in this respect fewest guarantees? Evidently the first condition of existence for our religious institutions of charity is sound doctrine. My readers, permit me to question you still more closely. Throw your eyes upon the eight or ten families best known to you, beginning with your own, and compare what they are now with what they were in 1819; contrast their occupations, tastes, sacrifices, and intercourse, the modes of education, the books read, friendships formed, and so on; and then declare, thankless ones, if God has allowed you to be without encouragement."*

M. Adolphe Monod had good reason to draw attention to this general progress of Christianity; but there was another progress also deserving notice, that which he had himself made, and which he was making more and more every day, in the attainment of the true and distinguishing character of a Christian.

At the commencement of his career as a minister of the Gospel, in his different controversies, and especially in his controversy with

* Pourquoi je demeure dans l'Église établie, par M. Adolphe Monod, pp. 25–32. Paris, 1849.

the Consistory of Lyons, he had shown rudeness, impatience, and want of foresight; he had been too precipitate in enforcing his faith by arguments, and too much disposed to undervalue the obstacles in its way. Thanks to his genuine sincerity and the natural elevation of his character, time, experience, and success had given at once breadth and suppleness to his thought. Faith had generated modesty, and hope patience. Contrary to the ordinary bias of men, his liberalism had increased in the same measure as his strength. As an act of duty he made in 1848 an avowal of the state of his mind in this respect. "The age," he said, "reproaches us with '*exclusisme*,' (exclusiveness,) a new word expressly invented to denote its favorite charge; for false ideas the age has only the resource of a barbarous phraseology. This '*exclusisme*' is the sole thing which the age cannot tolerate in matters of doctrine: it is prepared, it says to itself, to take everything within its pale except the 'exclusives.' Thus they demand from us only one change in the profession of our faith; they call upon us to substitute for our usual prefatory formula, 'This is the truth,' the words, 'This is my opinion.' And if they, in claiming such qualification of language, limited their demand to things which, in spite of any relative importance, do not constitute the substance of the faith and of the life of a Christian, we should do what they require; perhaps I should rather say, we do it already, as brother should do to brother, and in the interest of truth itself. It is one of the distinctive features of the awakening of Christians in our epoch, that charitably sparing in the absolute dogmatism of which the sixteenth century was prodigal, they make dogmas of only a small number of fundamental doctrines. And even of these they strive to contract the circle, until having reached the vital forces, the very heart, so to say, of truth, they sum it up in one single name, Jesus Christ, and in one single word, grace. Whoever is of that faith, whatever name he bears elsewhere, and whatever place he occupies in the Universal Church—Lutheran, Anglican, Methodist, Moravian, Baptist, nay, Roman Catholic, or Greek Catholic, we receive that man as a brother in Christ Jesus; and not we only, but the whole contemporary Evangelical Church, with certain exceptions becoming every day rarer, and arising from a narrow or sectarian pietism. Hence the 'Evangelical Alliance,' formed in our own time of more than twenty Protestant denominations, the prelude only to another evangelical alliance which will exclude none who rely upon the sole merits of Jesus Christ, the Saviour and Lord of all.

"Our '*exclusisme*,' besides, has not for its objects individuals but doctrines. Absolute affirmation is legitimate when the object is to define the faith, which is the promise of salvation, for God has clearly revealed it in his word; but when the object is to mark the individuals who possess that saving faith, similar affirmation could not be used without temerity; for God has nowhere revealed to us either the internal state of any man, or the final lot reserved for him. *We* exclude no man, *we* judge no man, alive or dead; the judgment of the quick and of the dead belongs to God alone. Doubtless we estimate, according to our ability, the spiritual condition of a man by his works, as we do a tree by its fruits; Jesus himself invites us to do so. Doubtless, when we see a man living and dying in the works of the faith, we hope for him, and our hope may grow even to a firm assurance; and when, on the contrary, we see a man living and dying in the works of incredulity, we have a feeling of anxiety for him—a feeling as painful as it is mysterious. But, after all, neither in the first case nor in the second, and still less in the second than the first, are we authorized to pronounce any personal judgment; and but for the paradoxical turn of the expression, I would willingly adopt the language of the devout Bunyan: Three things would astonish me in heaven; first, not to see there certain persons whom I expect to see there; secondly, to see there those I do not expect to see there; and thirdly, which would surprise me most, to see myself there.'"*

A piety so profound, and at the same time so modest and so large, expressed with an eloquence which combined an impassioned earnestness of language with an impassioned earnestness of conviction, could not fail to exercise great influence. As a preacher, M. Adolphe Monod was powerful. He had acquired, not by careful and cold observation, but by an

* Sermon sur l'Exclusisme, ou l'unité de la foi, in the Recueil des Sermons de M. Adolphe Monod. 3me série, t. ii, pp. 386–390. Paris, 1860. The sermons of M. Adolphe Monod have been collected and published in four vols. 8vo. Paris, 1856–1860. He also wrote several small works, among others:

1. Lucile, ou la lecture de la Bible. 1841.

2. La Destitution d'Adolphe Monod, récit inédit, rédigé par luimême. 1864.

3. Récit des conférences qui ont eu lieu en 1834, entre quelques Catholiques Romains et M. Adolphe Monod. Paris, 1860.

4. Les adieux d'Adolphe Monod à ses amis et à l'église. Paris, 1856.

assiduous and conscientious study of the Gospels and of himself, a remarkable knowledge of human nature, of its strength and of its weakness, of its deficiencies and of its aspirations. He laid siege, so to speak, to the souls of men, and he pressed the siege ardently and with skill; he assailed all their gates, and pursued them to their innermost defenses, keeping constantly displayed the banner of Christ, and inspiring them with the perfect confidence that he was urging them to take *their* stand, too, beneath it, not from any human motive, or any desire of glory to himself, but from a serious desire for their souls' welfare, and from it alone. Thus did he gain over to his Divine Master the hearts disposed to receive him, strongly shake the purpose of those not confirmed in their rebellion, and leave astonished and intimidated those whom he did not bring over. As pastor also his influence was extraordinary; his life was the reflection and the commentary upon his preaching. He applied first to his own case the precepts of his faith, and the conclusions therefrom logically deducible. As he said nothing that he did not think, so he thought nothing that he did not practice; and without being readily impressionable, like that of M. Vinet, his zeal was expansive, and his piety gave him no rest from the task of diffusing by example and precept the faith and the practice of Christianity. Attacked by a painful and incurable illness, which at last condemned him to immobility, he did not suffer it to render him inactive and useless. Every Sunday during the last six months of his life, his family, some pastors his colleagues, and as many attached friends as his chamber could receive, gathered around his bed, and his zeal surmounted his pain. He addressed to them, to use his very words, "sometimes the regret of a dying man, sometimes the results of his own experiences of faith and of life." The devout assemblage was again convoked, at his expressed wish, for the 6th April, 1856. But that day, before the hour fixed for the assembly had arrived, God took to him his servant, granting the wish expressed in his own often repeated prayer, "Let my life only terminate with my ministry, and my ministry only with my life."*

Eighteen months before the decease of M. Adolphe Monod, an eminent pastor of the Lutheran Church of Paris, his friend and fellow-laborer in the work of Christianity, M. Edouard Verny, died suddenly in the Evangelical Chair at Strasbourg, while preaching upon the words addressed by the Apostles to the Christians of Antioch, "It seemed good to the Holy Ghost, and to us, to lay upon you no greater burden than these *necessary* things," words not less liberal than pious, and faithfully expressing the sentiments of the Christian orator, who died while commenting upon them. The mind of M. Verny was naturally liberal and independ-

* These are the words inserted in a publication bearing the title "Les adieux d'Adolphe Monod à sa famille et à l'église," in which the last exhortations and conversations of this dying Christian have been piously collected. P. viii. Paris, 1856.

ent; his intellectual career had commenced with philosophical studies, and he had retained a strong bias in favor of the progress of thought. This did not, however, prevent him from promptly and calmly appreciating the opinions which he did not share. Without possessing either the impassioned style or the power of M. Adolphe Monod, he was not less devoted to the cause of Christianity; and he convinced those by the charms of his manner, into whose minds M. Monod entered by force and as a conqueror.*

* Although M. Verny had long preached, and had often written in religious reviews and journals, and particularly in the "Semeur," very few monuments remain of his ideas and of his talents. The principal are:

1. A sermon "Upon the Unity of the Church," preached in the church of Bolbec in 1854.

2. Two sermons, one "Upon the Prayer of the Canaanite Woman;" the other "Upon Repentance;" preached at Paris in 1843 and 1846.

3. The sermon "Sur l'Ouverture solennelle de la session du Consistoire supérieur de l'Eglise de la Confession d'Augsbourg," preached at Strasbourg on the 19th of October, 1854: while preaching which M. Verny died in the pulpit.

4. An "Essai sur les droits de la science," inserted in the

Although the Protestant Church of France thereby sustained an immense loss, it had a striking and salutary spectacle also presented to it by the end of these two servants of Christ, the one dying suddenly, in the plenitude of his strength, at the very moment when from his pulpit he was maintaining with distinguished ability the doctrines of his Master; the other, from his bed, gathering with pain what of breath remained to him in this world, to pour once more a flood of faith into the souls of his auditors.

Such lives, such deaths, could not remain sterile of result; under their influence the Christian faith was relumed; it again spread itself among the Protestants of France. Nor was this that arid cold faith which men accept to acquit their consciences, and to rid themselves

"Revue de Théologie et de Philosophie Chrétienne," published at Strasbourg by M. Colani. Vol. ix, pp. 208–248. 1854. This essay was to have been followed by an "Essai sur les devoirs de la foi," of which the sudden death of M. Verny prevented the completion.

of a trouble and a scruple; nor that vague and dreamy faith which feasts rather upon its own emotions, than nourishes itself with the truths which are the voice of God. A Christian's faith is neither an act of prudent submission nor a paroxysm of mystic fervor. Conviction and sentiment, the firm adhesion of the mind, and the filial love of the heart, meet in that faith in essential and intimate union. It is the light coming from on high, and bringing down with it the genial principles of vital warmth and fecundity; out of which, like salubrious waters from a pure source, flow freely and in abundance the works of human charity. I have lying before me a list of the different charities to which Christianity has in our own days since the reaction given birth in the Protestant Church of France.*

I see there manifold associations, enterprises

* Exposé des œuvres de la charité protestante en France, par H. de Triqueti, membre du conseil presbytéral et du diaconat de l'Eglise réformée de Paris. 18mo. 1863.

supposing a long duration of existence, unremitting efforts for the moral development of men; for the bodily solace of their earthly condition; for the propagation and the defense of freedom of opinion in religious matters; for the support and diffusion of the faith itself: all these objects, at once so various and so analogous, are being laboriously worked out both by the independent Protestant Churches, and by the Protestant Church established from the State. M. Edmond de Pressensé and M. Eugène Bersier devote their talents and their zeal to the same forms of Christian belief as were advocated by M. Alexandre Vinet and M. Adolphe Monod. In spite of the free divergence of sentiment and the diversity of ecclesiastical government in French Protestantism, we may observe in its bosom a progress of Christian Faith, a progress in works of Christian Charity, a progress in Christian Science, and a progress in Christian Influence. I use the same terms employed by me in speaking of the contemporary Catholic

Church of Rome, because I find before me similar facts. These facts do not announce the reconciliation of the two Churches—profound differences of opinion continue to separate them; but these facts are, in both Churches, signs of the Awakening of Christianity.

III. AWAKENING OF CHRISTIANITY IN FRANCE.

BUT the world has not changed since God at its creation delivered it up to the disputes of mankind; nor have the diversity and conflict of ideas and of passions ever ceased to be the condition of humanity. By the side of the movement of Christianity to which I refer, a movement in the contrary direction is manifesting itself, and is pursuing its course. Christianity at its Awakening is challenged to ruder combats. Philosophy refuses to its fundamental dogmas the marks and the rights of rational truth. An erudite criticism contests its historical evidence. The natural sciences proclaim that they do not require its aid to account for man and for the world. It is affirmed as a principle, and maintained in learned societies, that morality is entirely independent of religion. Man in his aspirations for liberty, that generous passion of the age, retains a profound resentment for the chains and the sufferings which, under pretext of Christianity, human conscience and human thought have so long been made to endure. The influence of these bitter reminiscences is manifesting itself in the different Christian Churches under various forms, and with different effects. Many liberals so dread the prospect of the Church of Rome obtaining power over civil society that they hardly accord to this Church the rights of common liberty; or, if they do so at all, they do it reluctantly and little by little.

Among the Protestants, some push the pretensions of liberty so far as to insist that in religious society a community of faith should count for nothing; that a man should be entitled to remain a member of a Church, and even to remain its minister, although he profess respecting the essential facts and dogmas of the Church the most contradictory opinions, and opinions the strangest to its traditions and its texts. With respect to Roman Catholics, the dominant question is that of liberty. Are the liberties of civil society to be accorded to the Church? Are those of the Church to be allowed to remain intact in the bosom of the State? In Protestantism, on the other hand, the complete liberty of religion in the midst of civil society, the right of every individual to avow his belief, and to solemnize his own forms of worship—these are all privileges already acquired, and contested as little by any orthodox believer as by any freethinker. The questions really here agitated are questions of faith and of discipline. Are a common faith and a uniform internal discipline essential to the Church? Here is the debate. But above all these special questions and these different situations of the various Christian Churches rise, for Romanist and Protestant alike, the general question and the common situation; it is Christianity itself which is engaged in the contest, and its awakening spirit confronts the antichristian movement.

Let us not delude ourselves as to the character, the force, or the danger of this antichristian movement. It is not merely a feverish excitability in men's minds, a simple revolutionary crisis in the religious order. No; we have here earnest convictions at work, and the prospect of a long war. Impatience of an ancient yoke, a spirit of reaction, a love of innovation, frivolous instincts not a few, as well as evil impulses, may claim a share—and a large share—in the attacks of which Christianity is in these days the object; but what gives to these attacks their most formidable character is a sentiment far more serious, one that has made heroes and martyrs, the love of truth at all risk and in despite of consequence, for the sake of truth and for its sake alone. The feeling that makes man thirst for truth is an honor to human nature. If he fancies that he has found that truth, man abandons himself with transport to the satisfaction of his cravings, and does not scruple to drink even to intoxication at this pure source. But here he is incurring a great danger: man is not merely an intelligence whose vocation during his brief transit through this world confines him only to study and science: he is an active, responsible being; a being engaged in a life full of labors, with a future life before him full of mystery; a laborer in a career having a particular interest for himself, and yet forming part of a general scheme, of the design of which he has but imperfect glimpses. Very incomplete and very imperfect is that man's state of intellectual action, who restricts himself to that which appears to him to be scientific truth, who does not, at the same time, submit his thought to all the tests to which he is himself subject, and who does not examine whether that thought be in harmony with the laws of his nature—whether it respect or transgress the limits imposed upon his means of knowledge. The danger of falling into error becomes greater in proportion as this incomplete and imperfect state of his mind is in itself a noble state, a state that satisfies noble impulses, and procures noble means of enjoyment. The most eminent among the actual adversaries of Christianity believe themselves the interpreters and the defenders of truth; some of philosophical truth; others of historical truth, others again of the truth of the facts and laws of the physical world. They are all proud of belonging to the department of pure science, and of making of scientific truth the sole object, the sole rule of their labors; but they are also all forgetful of some conditions—nay, the most indispensable ones—to which science is bound to conform; some tests—and the most legitimate ones—to which science is obliged to submit.

They claim, too, the honor of bearing the banner of a grand and noble cause, the cause of Liberty. That Christianity alone restored to man, as man, and for no other reason, his rights to liberty, is a fact that the comparative histories of the world, whether Christian or Pagan, place beyond all doubt; for confront these two histories, and name the nations among whom the idea of the dignity of man's liberty became a general idea, powerful in influence and fruitful in consequence! Another fact equally historic and certain is, that Christianity knew how to adapt itself, and did readily adapt itself, to the different states of society, and the different forms of government; that it set itself up and maintained its rank in republics as well as monarchies, under constitutional régimes as well as in despotisms, in the midst of democratical as well as aristocratical institutions; and, beyond doubt, it was not in free states that it displayed least vigor, or met with the smallest success. These two great facts are nowadays lost sight of. Christianity is accused of being hostile to Liberty and incompatible with the spirit of modern societies; and this is, indeed, the chief charge laid to its score. True it is, that the charge is not without deriving countenance from the history of Europe in modern times; worldly interests, selfish passions, events complex and obscure, in which moral order and social order have been compromised, have as it were suspended in certain countries the liberal action of Christianity, and enlisted momentarily the cause of Liberty under a banner not Christian. The error is profound, but transient; the traditional influences of ages will resume their empire, the grand events their course; Christ's religion and man's liberty will once more remember that each stands in need of the other, and that their alliance in the bosom of order is their natural and necessary condition. That they do misunderstand each other occasions the most serious crisis at this moment in modern society.

Here, too, is the gravest peril which the Christian religion has in our days to surmount. Appreciate the force of the two sentiments to which I just now referred, the love of science and the love of liberty; understand through what phases of degeneration and of deceptive transformation those sentiments may, in the ardor of pursuit and of combat, have to pass; reckon up, if reckon you can, all the false ideas, the chimerical hopes, which they may suggest; and then add to the amount, and as their consequences, the immoral and anarchical passions which may make those sentiments their pretext and their tools; and in doing this, you will find that you have passed in review the forces of that enemy now waging an implacable war against Christianity, although a war to which Christianity is called upon to put an end.

I do not in any respect underrate the forces of that army. I disparage no more their quality than their numbers. To maintain the combat worthily and efficaciously we should, at the onset, accord to our adversaries the whole amount of their merits as well as of their strength, and then attack them in their strongest entrenchments. I have charged the enemies of Christianity with puerile presumptousness when they refuse to see the energy and the progress of the awakening of Christianity. It is of infinite importance to Christians, on their side, not to be blind to the ardor and the effects which that Antichristian demonstration is producing, of which their Faith and their Church are the aim. I am firmly convinced that in this war Christianity will conquer; but it will leave its enemies with arms still in their hands. It will no more gain over them any complete or definitive victory than it will be able to conclude with them any serious or durable peace. In the actual state of men's minds and of society, the struggle will go on between the followers and the opponents of Christianity; the two armies will continue to deploy their forces in the face each of the other; and that of the

Christians, in order to defend and to extend its domain, will be incessantly called upon to watch and to combat the movements of its enemy. While combating them it will be also obliged to comply with the terms that truth exacts, and the conditions that liberty imposes. From these exigencies and these conditions Christianity has nothing to dread—that is, if it accepts them boldly, and in its turn imposes them upon its enemies. Let man's science, labors, and systems be submitted to the same tests, and handled with the same freedom of examination, as are being applied to the foundations and the doctrines of Christian faith; this is all that Christians are entitled to, all that they need to demand.

Thus far I have explained the actual state of the Christian religion in France, the sources of its strength and of its weakness, its awakening and its perils. It is my intention now to examine the actual state of those doctrines and systems which repudiate, or which more or less deny and combat Christianity. When I have passed the hostile army in review, I will once more confront Christianity with its adversaries, and endeavor to distinguish, by contrasting them, on which side the truth is, on which side the right, and on which side the hope of future success.

SECOND MEDITATION.

SPIRITUALISM.

I WITNESSED the birth—not, certainly, the birth of Spiritualism, for this was, like its twin brother Materialism, born in the cradle of Philosophy, and while the steps of Philosophy were still those of an infant—but the birth of the spiritualistic school of the nineteenth century. This birth was a national reaction against the Sensualism of the eighteenth century—just as the Christian Awakening was a reaction against the impiety of the same epoch. Theories do not escape the influence of events: after the ideas come the facts, to pour upon those ideas floods of light, and to reveal the vices, whether of philosophy or of policy, in all their practical consequences. The Sensualism—that is to say, to style it by its true name, the Materialism—of the eighteenth century, did not pass triumphantly through this test: it still reigned in France at the commencement of the nineteenth century, but it was the reign of an antiquated sovereign in decline—a sovereign of whom the public know the defects, and whose successor is at hand.

M. Royer-Collard was the first who had the merit and the honor of bringing back Spiritualism into the teaching of philosophy and into the minds of the people; his was a return simply to the spiritualistic doctrines of the seventeenth century; but still a real progress, effected by a novel route, and a really scientific method. M. Royer-Collard was neither a philosopher by profession nor the disciple of any master, nor was his mind a mind disposed to take up with systems—he observed, he read, he studied and reflected, as a looker on, and an earnest judge of the world and of men. In philosophy and his professional chair, as later in politics and in the chamber, he was an original and profound thinker. His mind united good sense with loftiness of sentiment, circumspection with self-respect; he was thoroughly imbued with the spirit of his times, at the same time that he refused to accept its yoke. In his grave and independent course of instruction, he treated philosophical questions as they presented themselves step by step, each on its own account, without troubling himself about anything but the discovery of the truth; and still less with any zealous endeavor to set together or resolve all the questions upon a general system, the result of any learned premeditation. Those who had opportunities of listening to him, and even those whose only means of judgment are the fragments published by M. Jouffroy,* characterize his lessons as directed, each of them, toward some special questions well determined beforehand, and they regard them as models of analysis and of philosophical criticism, scrupu-

*In his "Traduction des œuvres complètes de Reid," vol. iii, pp. 299–449, vol. iv, pp. 273–451.

lously confined by the lecturer to the facts and the results that the inductive process discovers in the facts themselves. He had been a great reader of the writings of the Scotch philosophers, held them in high esteem, and walked in their steps; his views were, however, loftier, and his footing firmer, although not less prudent. He had in his short philosophical career two rare pieces of good fortune: one was, that he had a friend in M. Maine de Biran, a profound and enthusiastic observer of the human soul in his own soul—a subtle metaphysician, almost a mystic, whom I would, if I dared, name the Saint Theresa of philosophy; his other advantage was, that he had for his disciple M. Cousin, the congenial rival and eloquent interpreter of the great philosophers of all ages. M. Cousin, in his turn, has been fortunate in having for his disciple M. Jouffroy—a disciple, of mind original and independent, following a master accomplished in the art of observing intellectual and moral facts, and of describing them and ordering them, without altering their essential character. Sometimes, it is true, M. Cousin yields to the ambition of his thought, or is swayed by the intellectual current of opinions in vogue; but very soon his common sense checks, or at least sets him on his guard—a common sense that finds lucid expression, and is distinguished by probity of intent. Such are the founders and the glorious chiefs of the spiritualistic school of the nineteenth century.

Nor have they failed to find disciples and heirs worthy of such predecessors. For some years past it has been the custom, in certain regions of the learned world, to demand, frivolously enough, and in a tone not free from irony, "What has become of the spiritualistic school —what can it be about?" I will not answer for it as Tertullian did to the Pagans, "We are only of yesterday, and we are everywhere— in your domains, your cities, your isles, your fortresses, your communes, your councils, your camps, your tribes, your 'decuries,' in the palace, the senate, the forum; we only leave you your temples.* The modern Spiritualists had no such conquests to make, and it is fitting for philosophers to be more modest; but however short my experience may have taught me that the human memory may in similar cases sometimes be, I am astonished that men should so forget facts, and facts, too, that are recent and patent. What school of philosophy ever furnished in half a century so many men and so many works, some of eminence, all of them of distinguished merit? I will cite only a few names: MM. de Rémusat, Damiron, Adolphe Garnier, Franck, Jules Simon, Barthélemy, Saint-Hilaire, Saisset, Caro, Bersot, Lévêque, Bouillier, Janet, some of whom have scarcely disappeared from the stage of the world, and others are only just arrived there—they belong all to the spiritualistic school, to which they have all done honor by important works on philosophy, whether speculative, historical, political, economic, or

* Tertullian Apologet., ch. xxxvii.

practical. Their doctrines, it is true, have now been for some time hotly attacked, and the wind of the day does not blow into their sails. They have, besides, in my opinion, been wrong in this respect, that they have not directed sufficient attention to these polemics; that they have combated in a manner too indirect, or with too little energy; the ideas in whose name their own have been assailed; a certain share of languor and of embarrassment is at this moment the malady of the best minds and of the sincerest convictions. But in spite of the blows which it receives and returns, although with insufficient sturdiness, the spiritualistic school, if we judge it by the names and the works which belong to it, by their talent, and their fame, remains in our century in possession of the domain and of the banner of philosophy.

Its merits will present themselves still more clearly if we examine closely the results of its labors.

The first and the most important result, in a

point of view purely philosophical, is, that the Spiritualists of our days have given to their researches and to their ideas a character really scientific: they have introduced into the study of man and of the intellectual world, the method practiced with so much success in the study of man and of the material world—that is to say, they have taken the observation of facts as the point of departure and the constant guide of their investigations. Are there in man and in the intellectual world, as there are in man and in the material world, facts capable of being observed, seized, described, classified, generalized? This is the question which the spiritualistic school proposed and discussed at the outset. I have no hesitation in saying, that it resolved it in the affirmative, and that, thanks to this school, psychology has assumed its rank among the positive sciences, just as physiology did. Like physiology, geology, or botany, psychology has its special object, its determined domain, in which it proceeds absolutely according to the same method observed by the physical sciences in their domain. That this method, the observation of facts, of their value and their laws, is in psychology more difficult to be followed than in the physical sciences, is certain; but this certainly does not deprive psychology either of its domain or of its scientific character. It is a science by the same right and upon the same conditions as all the others are so. The labors of the spiritualistic school, and particularly those of M. Jouffroy, have given it a solid foundation: and this has been formally recognized by several even among the adversaries of this school, among others by M. Taine and M. Berthelot.*

It is in the name of science and by the processes of science that the Spiritualists of the

*I read in the Métaphysique et la Science of M. Vacherot:

"*The Metaphysician:*

"In his denial of psychology, I stop at once the author of the 'positive philosophy,' and I demand of him by what right he thus banishes from the domain of the experimental sciences a science of observation.

"*The man of learning:*

"It constitutes in effect a 'hiatus' in this philosophy, and a nineteenth have combated the Sensualists of the eighteenth century. They have not, it is true, absolutely crushed Materialism, that child and legitimate heir of Sensualism; but while dethroning the parent, they have compelled the child sometimes to avow himself boldly, sometimes to transform himself, and to assume other features and other arms than those of his cradle. I will only cite the lecture of M. Cousin on the "Sensualistic Philosophy in the Eighteenth Century," and the essay of the Duke de Broglie on the "Existence of the Soul,"* written on the

hiatus which all the sound minds of the positive school are beginning to admit. M. Littré, for example, may make his reservations of opinion as to the manner in which our psychologists understand psychology, and as to the method which they apply to it; but he has too much sense not to admit that the intelligence—all that constitutes man's identity, the moral man—is the object of a peculiar study, of which many previous works have shown the possibility, and many practical results prove the high and vital interest."—Vacherot, la Métaphysique et la Science, vol. iii, p. 181.

*This essay, first inserted in 1828 in the Revue Française, has been reprinted in the "Ecrits et discours divers" of the Duke de Broglie, collected and published in 1863.

occasion of the work of M. Broussais: "De l'Irritation et de la Folie." Whoever, after having read them, would still persist in maintaining the Sensualism of Locke and of Condillac, or in refusing to see the consequences to which Sensualism leads, would prove, in my opinion, that he has not understood either the question put, or the doctrine combated and refuted. We have here a result acquired for the science of the intellectual world, and we owe the result to the polemics of the spiritualistic school.

That school has obtained another result more important still, and which belongs no longer to the polemics of simple negation, but to positive doctrine; it has set in the broad light of day the real and fundamental principle of morals, the distinction as to the essentials of moral good and evil, as well as the law of obligation, that "categorical imperative," the sole refuge which Kant found against Skepticism. Neither the interest well defined of each individual, nor the interest of the greater numbers, nor any sentimental sympathy, nor any system of positive written law, can, for the future, be considered as the basis of morals. An attempt is made in the present day to establish another thesis, and to represent morality as absolutely independent of religion. Grave error, which discards from morality, if not its principle, at least its source and its object, its author and its future; an error, however, very different from those errors which dispense even with the principle of morals, and assign as the rule for the conduct of men, motives having in themselves nothing moral, nothing absolute. The fact that man's conscience and man's reason recognize the distinction of moral good and evil, and at the same time the duty of practicing that good as the law of human actions, is a fact which we may now regard as acquired to philosophy. The treatise "Du Bien," in the work of M. Cousin upon "Le Vrai, le Beau, et le Bien," the preface of M. Jouffroy to the "Outlines of Moral Philosophy," by Dugald Stewart, and the "Essia sur la Morale," in the "Mélanges Philosophiques," which M. Jouffroy published in 1833, the book of M. Jules Simon upon "Le Devoir," these are all solid and brilliant works, by which the spiritualistic school has victoriously established the truth to which I have referred.

And in establishing it, it has paid a remarkable act of homage to another fact, and rendered an immense service by enforcing a truth, with which are intimately connected man's rights in this world, as well as his prospects beyond this world: I mean the fact of man's liberty. This is no question of pure theory and scientific curiosity; but a vital question, whose solution has for man, in time present and time future, the most important practical consequences. Upon what grounds would the claim of man to liberty in the social state rest, what would become of his hopes and fears of a future eternity, if man were not a being morally free and responsible for the decisions which determine his acts? The civil liberty of man during his life on earth, and his future destiny after his life on earth, closely depend upon the fact of his free volition and upon the responsibility which accompanies it. Without free volition man falls in this world, without rights, under the yoke of whatever force may take possession of him, or use him as its instrument; what remains for man, then, but to tremble at the destiny which awaits him beyond this world by virtue of the unknown decree of his Sovereign Master? To the spiritualistic school belongs the honor of having firmly established and rendered plain the psychological fact of the freedom of the human will; nor in doing so has it allowed itself to be troubled and blinded by the ontological questions which that fact suggests, or by the difficulty attending the solution of these questions. Consequently, it has accepted upon this point the limits of man's science, and at the same time maintained the rights of man's nature. It has laid in man's liberty and man's responsibility the legitimate foundation of political liberty, as well as that of the personal morality of man and of man's future.

Thus, then, the spiritualistic school of the nineteenth century is at once scientific, moral, liberal. Eminent merits, rare combination in any time, and still more so in our time!

With these great merits, and in spite of them, two omissions are still remarkably striking.

The spiritualistic school, our contemporary, has halted abruptly before the sovereign problems which weigh upon the human soul, and which, in the first series of these "Meditations," I styled natural problems;* it has in no respect furthered their solution according to reason, or accepted their solution according to Christianity; its "Theodicy" has remained far in arrear of its Psychology. Halted it has, also, before any practical solution of these same problems; nor has it eliminated either any faith or any law which suffices for man's soul or man's conduct in life—in short, any religion.

* Meditations on the Essence of the Christian Religion.

M. Jules Simon, in his work entitled "La Religion Naturelle," MM. Saisset and De Rémusat, in their "Essais de Philosophie Religieuse," have striven, irrespectively of all positive revelation, to give to man's soul and to man's conduct that satisfaction and that religious rule which both require. I doubt their counting much upon the success of their attempts; I doubt their believing that their natural religion, or their religious philosophy, are sufficient substitutes for Christianity. Far other things than such drops of science are required to appease the thirst of humanity for religion.

Whence, in the spiritualistic school, this double hiatus—this twofold weakness, whence?

In my opinion, the causes are themselves twofold. The spiritualistic school has been at once too timid and too proud. It has not seen in the psychological facts which it was observing and describing, all that they contain and reveal upon the subject of the great natural problems of man and of the world; it has neglected the cosmological facts and the historical facts which concur to throw light upon those problems; its psychology has remained isolated and incomplete. It has, at the same time, failed to see the limits of psychology and of human science in general; not having succeeded in advancing the torch of science into the regions where access to it is denied, it has refused to accept the light descending upon man by another way than that of science.

Like Plato, Descartes, Leibnitz, Reid, and Kant, M. Cousin, now the most eminent representative of the spiritualistic school, establishes, by virtue of psychological observation, these two great facts: first, that there exist universal and necessary principles manifesting themselves in the human mind, and reigning there without being capable of being subverted, which are called into action by sensations coming from the external world; secondly, that these sensations, so coming from the external world, do not in any way supply the human mind with these universal and necessary principles, and that they can explain neither their presence nor their origin. Such, for instance, are the principles, that everything which begins to appear has a cause—that every quality belongs to a substance!* Sensualism is not in a position to account in any way for these two principles, or to find them among those facts that form all its psychology.

I am not called upon to develop or to discuss this idea, which, for my part, I fully admit; enough that I mention it as a fundamental doctrine of the spiritualistic school.

The philosophers, who have admitted the existence of these universal and necessary principles, have assigned them different names, and have enumerated and classified them differently; but whether they style them "ideas," or "innate ideas," or "laws," or "forms," or "categories of the understanding"—whether they enlarge or limit their number—they agree as to their

* Du Vrai, du Beau, et du Bien, pp. 19–66. 1857.

nature, and declare them inherent in the human mind itself, which applies them, so to say, as its own peculiar property in its appreciation of the external world; so far is the mind from borrowing them from that world!

These universal and necessary principles once admitted and characterized, some of the philosophers who so admit and characterize them, the Scotch philosophers for instance, go no further, and adhere to the psychological fact without examining its value or its consequences in an ontological sense. Others, like Kant, refuse to that psychological fact all ontological value, and are of opinion that nothing authorizes us in affirming that those principles, inherent in the internal existence of the human mind, are true in the domain beyond the human mind, or that they regulate the realities of the external world, as they regulate our intellectual activity. Others, finally, M. Cousin, with Plato, Descartes, Leibnitz, Fénélon, and Bossuet, see the work of God, and consequently God himself, in the universal and necessary principles which preside over the intellectual existence of man; and they recognize God as the infinite and sovereign being in whom the necessary principles reside; and they regard these as the manifestations of him, and think that he placed them in the intelligence of man when he placed man himself in the middle of the world.

To this doctrine I firmly adhere; but why does the spiritualistic school so stop short, why does it not advance to the very end of the path upon which it has entered? It admits God as the being in whom these necessary principles reside, and from whom man has received them; what does this mean but that it recognizes in God the author and instructor of man? And to recognize in God the author and the instructor of man, what is this but to recognize the fact of the creation, and the fact of the primitive revelation inherent in the fact of the creation? These two truths are involved in the fact that the necessary principles exist in the mind of man, and that man derives them, not from his relations with the external world, but from himself, and from the source whence he himself emanates—from God, his Creator. God has created man armed at all points, as well in the order of the intellect as of matter, complete in his soul as in his body: that is to say, God has given to him at his creation the necessary principles of his intellectual life, just as he has given him the necessary mechanism of his physical organization. Scientific psychology thus mounts up to that supreme point where it meets Christian revelation. There is, on its part, inconsistency or timidity in not recognizing and proclaiming the existence of that light to which it so attains.

What was the import, what the form, of that primitive revelation? Has the revelation itself been renewed at any epoch subsequent to the creation? If so, by what instruments and with what incidents has it been renewed? These are questions to which I shall recur, but which for the moment I do not approach; I wish here only to establish the fact of the divine revelation in the sphere and in the terms of scientific psychology.

Facts in cosmogony lead to the same conclusion. I repeat here what I said in the first series of these Meditations, when speaking of the dogma of the creation:

"The only serious opponents of the dogma of the creation are those who maintain that the universe, the earth, and man upon the earth, have existed from all eternity, and, collectively, in the state in which they now are. No one, however, can hold this language, to which facts are invincibly opposed. How many ages man has existed on the earth is a question that has been largely discussed, and is still under discussion. The inquiry in no way affects the dogma of the creation itself; it is a certain and recognized fact that man has not always existed on the earth, and that the earth has for long periods undergone different changes incompatible with man's existence. Man, therefore, had a beginning: man has come upon the earth."*

He did not come there by spontaneous generation—that is to say, by any creative force or organizing power inherent in matter. Scientific observation overturns more and more, every day, this hypothesis, which, in other respects also, it is impossible to admit as any explanation of the first appearance upon the earth of the complete man, the man in a condition to survive. "Another delusion of which we must rid ourselves," said, lately, a member of the Academy of Sciences, as he quitted the lecture-room where M. Pasteur had been throwing upon this subject the light of his luminous and scrupulous criticism. The hypothesis of the progressive transformation of species does not explain better the existence of man, such as we now see him upon the earth. This hypothesis is also rejected by the exact student of facts;

*Meditations on the Essence of the Christian Religion, page 18.

even if admitted, it would still leave existing the same problems; for, whence came these primitive types, whose successive transformations have, as supposed, produced the existing species? God is as necessary to create the ape or the primitive type of the ape as he is necessary to create man himself. Scientific cosmology accords with scientific psychology. God, the creator and instructor of man, is the grand fact which each of these sciences encounters at the summit of its labors.

The whole current of history contains the same teaching. I admit that error abounds in history, that it is full of false assertions, of recitals tortured from the truth, facts mutilated, legends invented by men as imaginations. It is not, for all that, the less certain that in a great part the truth still remains there, that certain historical events are authenticated and attested by undeniable testimony. I mention here only two, because connected with the subject which engages me. It is a general belief, a universal tradition in the history of nations, that, either at the moment of the creation, or at some epoch subsequent to creation, the God, or the gods, whom those nations respectively adored, had had direct relations with man; had become manifest to him by different acts or under different forms, and had assumed a place and exercised an active influence upon man's destinies. The idea of a single revelation, or of a succession of revelations—revelations characterized at one time by a strange grossness, at another by a subtle mysticism, is a thing ever recurring in the history of humanity. The tradition of the special revelation, proclaimed first by the Hebrews, and after them by the Christians, is equally undeniable; criticism may apply itself to the volumes that contain the accounts; may contest the authenticity or exactitude or date of particular books; but so far from ever negativing, it will not even weaken the evidence of the existence and the powerful influence of the religious tradition which gave birth to Judaism and to Christianity. We have here a remarkable historical fact, manifesting at once the natural faith of mankind in the divine revelation, and in the relations of the Creator with his creatures.

If the spiritualistic school refused from its very origin to admit these facts, drawn from cosmogony and from man's history, into the sphere of its labors; if it limited psychology to its peculiar scientific object—the study of the human soul—I am far from making such refusal matter of reproach: for the Spiritualists did thereby nothing but what they were entitled and called upon to do. But they have fallen into a twofold error. While observing and describing psychological facts, they did not perceive nor accept all that they imported: they saw in the intelligent man the work and the trace of God; but they did not see what was implied in that man besides—that is, revelation as well as creation. They did not leave pure psychology to demand of kindred sciences, such as cosmology and history, whether their results accorded or did not accord with the results that they had deduced from psychology. In short, on the one side they stopped short of the limits of the domain of psychology; and on the other, they confined themselves to it too exclusively.

From this twofold error sprang another still more serious. Spiritualism gave birth to Rationalism—a transformation as unnatural as unfortunate, which has rendered the science of man and of the intellectual world still more inexact and incomplete!

THIRD MEDITATION.

RATIONALISM.

A man of a mind as unprejudiced as rare, one who will never be suspected of any undue bias for Christianity, M. Sainte-Beuve, avowing to me recently the high esteem with which M. Alexandre Vinet inspired him, borrowed an expression of Pascal's: "The heart has its reasons, which the reason does not comprehend."*

I only admit half of what is implied in this conciliatory phrase; and these are my reasons.

True religious faith, or, to call things by their real names, Christian faith, is founded

* Between this phrase and that of Pascal there is a slight difference. Pascal said, "Le cœur a des raisons que la raison ne connaît point:" "The heart has reasons that the reason knows not at all." Pensées de Pascal, edition of M. Faugère, 1844, vol. ii, p. 172.

upon instincts and upon sentiment at the same time that it is founded upon reasons. If reason do not accept the sentiments of the heart, on which side is the fault? Is the fault with the heart, that it feels them, or is it with the reason, that it does not comprehend them?

My reply to this question is easy. I reject the distinction made. I admit no such persons as are respectively styled the heart, the reason. Here is only an attempt at a psychological anatomy; no true enunciation of a real fact. Man, the human being, is essentially one, and single: he has the faculty of self-observation and self-study, but in exercising it he does not destroy the unity of his nature; it is not his mere reason, it is himself, and his whole self, that makes himself the object of his observation and of his study, and that cannot but recognize himself and accept himself in his entirety. He has no right to say, with an air of scientific disdain, "My reason comprehends not the reasons of my heart." He must perforce say: "I comprehend not myself;" he must perforce proclaim, not the incoherency of his being, but the insufficiency or the incompetency of what he styles his reason.

Philosophy, like poetry, is full of personifications that mislead; the one personifies by images, the other by abstractions. Both have need of them—the one for its creations, the other for its studies; I am far from seeking to deny their respective use. All that I contend for is, that we must not misconceive the real import of these expedients of human language; we must not, by taking them for realities, lose sight of or destroy what are really and genuinely realities, the entities of divine creation.

I insist the more on this error, because in the philosophy of our time it is a common and a potent error, and the source too of other errors, deplorable as well in a scientific as in a moral and practical point of view. Condillac and his disciples had set apart and specially studied in man the faculty of sensation, and they were thereby led to make out of this faculty, and out of it alone, man himself and the whole man. Kant and his school considered particularly in man the faculty of the reason and judgment, and very soon reason came with them to constitute the whole man. I am far from intending to examine in its fundamental principles and its entirety the system of Kant, the greatest philosophical work upon the human understanding that any man has produced since the time of Plato. I single out this fact, that it treats the reason as the proper, special, and paramount object of philosophy. Warned by his profound, scrupulous genius, Kant did not limit himself to a point of view so narrow, although so lofty; he studied man's reason under its different aspects, he constituted himself the critic of pure reason, the critic of practical reason, the critic of æsthetic reason—that is, of reason applied to the discrimination of the beautiful; he decomposed, so to say, the reason itself into as many different faculties as he found different phases in the intellectual and moral life of man; but the faculty that he styled the reason remained the basis of his study and of his system. It became in his school, and in the schools akin to it, pre-eminently the intellectual substance, the basis of man and of philosophy; and the human being himself, in his personal unity, with all his life and his free will, entirely disappeared from their teaching.

As results of this system I will cite only two facts, very different in their nature, both very foreign to the founder of the system and his disciples, but which serve the better to reveal that system's faultiness, as these facts are, although its indirect, remote, and involuntary, nevertheless, its undeniable consequences.

When, in 1793, the frenzied men who disposed, as masters, of the destinies of France, abolished the Christian religion and Christian worship, they resolved, nevertheless, to give to men an object to adore. They instituted the worship of reason. The church of Notre-

Dame at Paris was metamorphosed into a temple of reason; a young woman was made to figure there as the goddess of reason; and the orator of the National Convention, Chaumette, cried aloud as he pointed her out to the people, "Behold living Reason; we celebrate here to-day the sole true worship, the worship of Liberty and of Reason."

At the distance of three quarters of a century from the date of these revolutionary orgies, in 1865, not in France but in England, a man of earnest intentions, superior mind, and extensive learning, whose sincerity is evident, and his sentiments moral at once and moderate, writes a book entitled, "Rationalism in Europe;" and the object of this book is to establish, that all the good effected in Europe since the fall of the Roman empire, all the progress made by states in justice, in humanity, in liberty, and general happiness—whether in the sphere of science or of practical industry—is due to the influence of Rationalism, to its developments and its conquests. Mr. Lecky is not a metaphysician; he attaches no precise and philosophical meaning to the word "Rationalism;" he does not trouble himself about the system of Kant, nor the place occupied in it by the pure, the practical, or the æsthetic reason; he only retraces the intellectual and social history of Europe, and all the happy results that this history commemorates, all the salutary consequences of the activity of the human mind, of the liberty of man's thought, of the amelioration of human institutions and manners, he sums up all in a single name, attributes them to a single cause, and assigns all the honor to the progress of Rationalism!

Arrived, nevertheless, at the conclusion of his work, a single reflection disquiets Mr. Lecky: he asks himself whether, in extolling the happy effects of what he styles Rationalism, he has not gone too far, said too much, and hoped too much: "Utility is perhaps the highest motive to which reason can attain. . . . It is from the moral or religious faculty alone that we obtain the conception of the purely disinterested. . . . The substitution of the philosophical conception of truth for its own sake, for the theological conception of the guilt of error, has been in this respect a clear gain; and the political movement which has resulted chiefly from the introduction of the spirit of Rationalism into politics, has produced, and is producing, some of the most splendid instances of self-sacrifice. On the whole, however, the general tendency of these influences is unfavorable to enthusiasm, and both in actions and in speculations this tendency is painfully visible. With a far higher level of average excellence than in former times, our age exhibits a marked decline in the spirit of self-sacrifice, in the appreciation of the more poetical or religious aspect of our nature. The history of self-sacrifice during the last eighteen hundred years has been mainly the history of the action of Christianity upon the world. Ignorance and error have, no doubt, often directed the heroic spirit into wrong channels, and have sometimes even made it a cause of great evil to mankind; but it is the moral type and beauty, the enlarged conception and persuasive power of the Christian faith, that have chiefly called it into being, and it is by their influence alone that it can be permanently sustained. . . .

"This is the shadow resting upon the otherwise brilliant picture the history of Rationalism presents. The destruction of the belief in witchcraft and of religious persecutions; the decay of those ghastly notions concerning future punishments, which for centuries diseased the imaginations and embittered the character of mankind; the emancipation of suffering nationalities; the abolition of the belief in the guilt of error, which paralyzed the intellectual, and of the asceticism which paralyzed the material progress of mankind, may be justly regarded as among the greatest triumphs of civilization; but when we look back to the cheerful alacrity with which, in some former ages, men sacrificed all their material and intellectual interests to what they believed to be right, and when we realize the unclouded assurance that was their reward, it is impossible to deny that we have lost something in our progress." *

But to leave England and Mr. Lecky, and to return once more to France. I turn to the pages of a rationalistic philospher more profound, and more profoundly troubled, too, in his sentiments than Mr. Lecky. I find there, in an essay of M. Edmond Scherer, entitled "The Crisis of Protestantism,"† the following passage:

"That which is really imperiled is not so much Protestantism; it is Christianity, it is very religion. As for natural religion, that exists only in books. Religions which have vital force and influence are positive religions; that is, religions which have a Church, and particular

* History of the Rise and Influence of the Spirit of Rationalism in Europe, by W. E. H. Lecky, vol. ii, 1866, third edition, pp. 403–409.

† Mélanges d'histoire religieuse. Pp. 250–254. 1864.

rites, and dogmas. What are these dogmas? Taken in their intimate meaning, they are the solutions of the great problems which have ever disquieted the mind of man—the origin of the world, and of evil; the expiation; the future of humanity. The doctrines of religion are a sort of revealed metaphysics.

"Considered in its form, dogma is the supernatural—not merely because religions were born at an epoch when the imagination was greedy of miracles, and when the imagination, in her *naïveté*, associated herself with everything; but also because, as may be readily understood, it is impossible for a positive religion to have any other origin than a revelation; it is necessarily a history of the intervention of God in the destinies of man, the account of acts by which God created and saved the world—it is that or it is nothing. We see then at once that in religion everything is not religious. There is in every religion a multitude of elements, historical, physical, and metaphysical, as to which its dogmas may come into conflict with science. Nevertheless, it is not of this antagonism that I would here speak. The religious sentiment has also its critical action; *it* also may enter into a struggle with religion.

"As long as the authority of the priest or of the book preserves its prestige, the believer receives his religion ready made for him, without himself making distinctions; but as soon as that authority is shaken, a man, if he do not entirely reject his first belief, will at least no longer accept it without reservations. He only retains so much of it as enlightens or touches him, so much as commends itself to his understanding or to his heart; so much, in a word, as gives a satisfaction to his religious requirements.

"Thus it is that religious sentiment becomes the measure of religious truth. It receives all in religion that addresses itself to the soul, all that nourishes and fortifies the soul, all that raises the soul to the infinite and the ideal, all that unites the soul to God. Religious sentiment appropriates it all, but it appropriates nothing more. Let but a thing become indifferent, and it feels it as an importunity, and looks upon it in the light of an element strange, useless, arbitrary. It rejects, for this reason, doctrines purely speculative as well as facts purely marvelous. Man requires his religion to be entirely religious; that is to say, to be in all respects in direct relation with piety, and, so to speak, to be vertical to his conscience. The more his faith purifies itself, the more a man eliminates from his religion dogmas which, having no root either in the divine nature or man's nature, appear on that very account to have no ground to exist at all.

"At first sight this gradual emancipation of faith and this corresponding progress of religion in the ways of Spiritualism, seem a natural process by means of which religious opinion and the human mind contrive to maintain themselves in a state of constant equilibrium. We imagine all difficulties removed, and fancy that we catch a glimpse of the religious future of humanity in a sort of Christian Rationalism, a rational Christianity not excluding fervor of devotion, but leaving all its liberty to man's thought.

"I demand nothing better as far as I am concerned; but I cannot refrain from asking, not without anxiety, whether Christian Rationalism is really a religion. What remains in the crucible after the operation just detailed? Is the residue really the essence of the positive dogmas, or is it but a *caput mortuum?* When Christianity is rendered translucent to man's mind, conformable to man's reason and man's moral appreciation of things, does it still possess any great virtue? Does it not very much resemble Deism, and is it not equally lean and sterile? Does not the potent influence of religious belief reside in its dogmatic formulas and marvelous legends just as much as in anything more essentially religious that it possesses? Is there not even somewhat of superstition in genuine piety, and is it possible for piety to dispense with that popular system of metaphysics, that attractive mythology, which men strive to eliminate from it? Do not the elements which you pretend to abstract from religion constitute the alloy, without which the precious metal becomes unsuitable for the rough usages of life? In short, when criticism shall have succeeded in overthrowing the supernatural as useless, and dogmas as irrational; when the religious sentiment on the one side, and a scrupulous reason on the other, shall have penetrated man's belief, assimilated and transformed it; when no other authority shall remain standing, save that of the personal conscience of each individual; when, in a word, man having torn every vail and penetrated every mystery, shall behold that God face to face to whom he aspires, will it not be discovered that that God is, after all, nothing else than man himself, the conscience and the reason of humanity personified? Will not religion, in the very attempt to become more religious, have ceased to exist?"

Such, according to the views of its most eminent representatives, are the potent influences and the final results of Rationalism. After having confusedly attributed to it all the progress of man's thought and of man's civilization, Mr. Lecky expresses the apprehension that he has lowered the nature of man, by depriving him (these are his very words) "of our noblest quality, of the divine spark, the principle in us of everything that is heroic," the complete and pure devotedness of Christian faith. M. Scherer asks himself sadly if in rejecting all dogma and all positive revelation, in obliging religious sentiment to be self-sufficing, and to feed itself with its own and single virtue, rational criticism does not inflict a deadly blow upon religion itself; and M. Sainte-Beuve, in the same perplexity, contents himself with saying, as resignedly, though more coldly, "The heart has its reasons, which the reason comprehends not."

Nothing is so affecting to me, but nothing, at the same time, throws such light upon the subject of my meditations as this involuntary, this invincible anxiety observable in men of lofty sentiments and profound convictions, when confronting the chasms in their system, and dealing with the incoherences of their own convictions. However profound, however different my own conviction may be, I have no desire to engage, either with them or against them, in any direct or prolonged controversy. I have been engaged all my life in frequent and ardent polemics. Those could not be well avoided by a man like myself, forced not merely to combat human opinions, but to grapple with human affairs; and called upon to resolve, upon the instant, practical and urgent questions. But while I voluntarily submitted to the necessity of precipitate and unforeseen struggles, experience has taught me their inconveniences and their perils. The combatants on each side are prone to make use of weapons of too offensive a nature; men involve themselves for party interests and party honor, and push their conclusions with obstinate pertinacity beyond the strictness of truth, sometimes even beyond their own intentions. I do not wish in the arena of philosophy to run the risk of striking upon any similar rock; but avoiding all personal polemics, all controversy of detail, I will express upon the essence of Rationalism, although only in a general manner, my sincere and intimate convictions.

There are in Rationalism two fundamental errors. First, it mutilates man while it studies him; it holds as of no account several of the constituent elements and essential facts of human nature, of which it ignores the meaning and the import. Secondly, Rationalism extends the pretensions of human science beyond its rights, and beyond its legitimate limits.

The instincts, the sentiments, of humanity are certainly not sufficient reasons for scientific conviction, nor conclusive proofs in support of any particular system whatever. The instinctive belief of the human race in one or more supernatural forces is no demonstration of the reality of the supernatural; and the aspirings of man's soul for a life beyond this terrestrial one does not rationally prove the soul's immortality. Error may occur in human instincts or sentiments just as much as in human ideas. But when these instincts and these sentiments are universal, permanent, indestructible, encountered in all ages and in all countries—when they resist and survive all attacks, all doubts of reason or science—they are, beyond all question, considerable facts, and facts which the human understanding cannot but recognize and respect. If these instincts and sentiments do not solve the problems which trouble man's understanding, at least they demand imperiously some solution; if they throw no light upon his road to science, they oblige him to see that that road has its mysteries. Rationalism mutilates humanity when it ignores such facts, regarding them as vain illusions because it cannot explain them; and when, after this mutilation, it assigns the entire empire to a single portion of the human nature, to a single faculty, called by it reason, as if reason constituted the entire man, Rationalism does in the intellectual world what it would be doing in the physical world did it deny the reality of night because it only sees the day clearly.

Rationalism is the more wrong in thus discarding facts which it does not explain, that in its proper domain similar facts occur, and that its science of reason arrives also finally at mysteries. I mentioned it before, as a truth acquired to philosophy, that there exist in the human mind certain universal and necessary principles, neither furnished to the mind by impressions derived from the external world, nor created by the mind itself; and that those principles are inherent in the nature of the mind, and come to it from another source than that of sensation, or any discovery of man's own thought. We have here a psychological fact which, after the profound studies of the spiritualistic school from the time of Plato down to M. Cousin, Rationalism is obliged to admit. To what does this fact tend, and what is its logical consequence? What but God, creation, revelation, and the relations of God with man? Will Rationalism give any better explanation of these divine laws of the human mind than it has given of the instincts and of the sentiments of the human heart? or will it ignore the one result as it has ignored the other?

But now to touch upon the radical and permanent error of Rationalism. It regards all things as accessible to the researches and to the methods of human science. When Spiritualism has recognized and proclaimed the essential and necessary facts which constitute the intellectual and moral being by it styled man, it halts abruptly; it hesitates also to recognize and proclaim the mysterious facts in that sanctuary the very door of which it has reached; it does not resign itself to adore what lies behind the vail; it is inconsequent and timid, although respectful and modest. Rationalism, on the contrary, is presumptuous and audacious; its ambition is to see clearly, to touch what is in the center of the sanctuary, as it sees and touches what is on its outside. Its pretension is that it may study and know, by its ordinary processes, as well the invisible world, its Sovereign and its laws, as the visible world in which man is now placed; and it wars upon Christianity because Christianity admits no such pretension. But Christianity here encounters another adversary, Positivism. Positivism arrests its progress, saying: "I do not know, nobody knows, if an invisible world be or be not a really existing thing. It is a mere loss of time to think of it, for nothing can be known about it with certainty. All religion, all metaphysics, are chimerical and vain sciences; there is no science but the science of the physical world, of its facts and of its laws!"

FOURTH MEDITATION.

POSITIVISM.

I SEEK no quarrel with words, even when they provoke it. Positivism is a word, in language a barbarism, in philosophy a presumption. Unlike Geology, Ideology, Theology, Physics, it qualifies a doctrine, not by its object, but by its supposed merit. All science pretends to positiveness—that is, to be founded upon fact and truth. But "Positivism" alone arrogates to itself this quality. It is an arrogance, in my opinion, radically unjustifiable.

I knew its founder, M. Auguste Comte, personally. I had some communication with him in the period from 1824 to 1830. I then was struck by the elevation of his sentiments and by the vigor of his mind. In October, 1832, at the moment when I was entering upon my functions as Minister of Public Instruction, he came to me and formally demanded that I should create for him in the "College of France" a professorship of general history for the physical and mathematical sciences. I see no cause to express myself here otherwise than I have already done in my "Memoirs" as to the impression produced upon me by his conversation and his personal bearing. "He explained to me drearily and confusedly his views upon man, society, civilization, religion, philosophy, history. He was a man single-minded, honest, of profound convictions, devoted to his own ideas, in appearance modest, although at heart prodigiously vain; he sincerely believed that it was his calling to open a new era for the mind of man and for human society. While listening to him, I could hardly refrain from expressing my astonishment that a mind so vigorous should at the same time be so narrow as not even to perceive the nature and bearing of the facts with which he was dealing, and the questions which he was authoritatively deciding; that a character so disinterested should not be warned by his own proper sentiments—which were moral in spite of his system—of its falsity and its negation of morality. I did not even make any attempt at discussion with M. Comte: his sincerity, his enthusiasm, and the delusion that blinded him, inspired me with that sad esteem that takes refuge in silence. Had I even judged it fitting to create the chair which he demanded, I should not for a moment have dreamed of assigning it to him."*

I should have been as silent and still more sad if I had then known the trials through which M. Auguste Comte had already passed. He had been, in 1823, a prey to a violent attack of mental alienation, and in 1827, during a paroxysm of gloomy melancholy, he had

* "Mémoires pour servir a l'histoire de mon temps," t. iii, pp. 125–7. In the sixth volume of these Mémoires I have rectified an error inadvertently committed by me as to the epoch of my first relations with M. Auguste Comte.

thrown himself from the Pont des Arts into the Seine, but had been rescued by one of the king's guard. More than once, in the course of his subsequent life, this mental trouble seemed upon the point of recurring.

Many will be tempted to demand how a man so little master of himself, and whose mind was under so little government, could ever have succeeded in producing a doctrine so considerable, and in exercising such real influence upon the philosophical world. The fact is nevertheless beyond question. Whether the cause is to be referred to the merit of M. Comte and of his doctrine, or to the state of men's minds at the time, it is certain that not only in France but in Europe, and particularly in England, numerous and honorable disciples came over to his ideas, and that Positivism became a school wanting neither in sincerity nor credit. When such men as M. Littré, at Paris, and Mr. J. Stuart Mill, in London, declare themselves his adherents, the doctrine has claims to a serious examination.

M. Auguste Comte lived constantly, as far as he was individually concerned, under the empire of a fixed idea, which occasioned him many a painful disappointment; and he lived, as far as his system was concerned, under the empire of a false idea, which associated with views just in themselves and sometimes grand, one pervading and permanent error.

His fixed personal idea consisted in his thinking himself called to regenerate human science and human society by the single virtue of his doctrine. Besides their share in the presumptuousness which is the common character of mankind, minds that are inventive and fond of systematizing are particularly prone to extend beyond their legitimate bearings—nay, beyond all bounds—the pretensions and the hopes which their ideas suggest. M. Auguste Comte was one of the most striking instances, as well as one of the most honest victims, of this intellectual intoxication—the noblest although not the least fantastic form of human pride. The

Christian religion has its apostles and it has its missionaries, speaking in the name of a Master other than themselves, and preaching a faith they did not themselves originate. M. Auguste Comte was his own proper apostle—the inventor and missionary of his own proper faith. Of profound convictions, with no selfish, worldly views, he aspired to the entire empire of the intellect, believing both the interests of social order and the honor of the human mind involved in the triumph of his doctrine; he ardently desired not only its propagation, but its organization as a permanent and potent institution, to insure and perpetuate his triumph. The real and practical government of nations, according to him, was only, as it ought to be only, a sort of stewardship, charged with the duty of realizing and carrying into effect the ideas of thinking men. "The systematic separation of the two elementary forces, the Spiritual and the Temporal," so he wrote to Mr. J. Stuart Mill, "constitutes certainly the principal condition for a *dénouement* of the actual situation. I admit that the special requirements of a situation where those two forces are confounded may authorize, and sometimes oblige, philosophers, in the interest of a final regeneration, to participate, by way of exception, in actual political life, although an inclination for such a life exposes them to the danger of many a quicksand, and demands that their principles should be firmly settled, to avoid the risk of a real deviation. To embody my thought upon this subject in a palpable example relative to a great occurrence, I blame the philosopher Condorcet for having suffered himself to be returned as member to our glorious Convention, in which men of action were leaders, and properly so, whereas Condorcet could never be so placed as to regard things from the same point of view; hence that false position for which in the sequel he had so cruelly to suffer. But on the contrary, I should have regarded it as very natural for him to develop a great activity in the club of the Jacobins; for, placed beyond the sphere of the government, properly so called, that club constituted at that time a sort of spiritual power, in that remarkable and so little comprehended combination of things which characterized the revolutionary régime. . . . I have learned with much satisfaction," he added, still addressing Mr. Mill, "that the wise energy of your resistance has succeeded in triumphing over the blind persistence of your friends who urge you toward a parliamentary career. I shall propose in my last volume, and in direct terms, the institution, by individual efforts, of an European committee, charged permanently with the direction of a common movement of philosophical regeneration, when once Positivism shall have planted its standard—that is, its lighthouse, I should term it—in the midst of the disorder and confusion that reigns; and I hope that this will be the result of the publication of my work in its complete state." *

* Letters of the 20th November, 1841, and 4th March, 1842, published in the work of M. Littré, entitled, "Auguste Comte and the Positive Philosophy," pp. 424, 425, 427, 429.

One can scarcely refrain from a smile when he contemplates these dreams reduced to the form of system, ignoring every sentiment of reality, and expounded with the confidence of fanaticism in the name of a science called Positive. Here it is that we find the fixed and dominant idea that pervaded and compromised the whole life of M. Auguste Comte. Whoever did not accept his doctrine and his system, was for him either a retrogradist full of prejudice, or an ignoramus without scientific education, or an interested and jealous enemy. Whoever, on the other hand, lent himself to his views on any point, or for any time, however short, became in the eyes of M. Comte his conquest and his property, his philosophical serf, as it were, bound to his master by the tenure of duty, and the render of services from which he could never hope to enfranchise himself, without the risk of being treated upon the instant as a deserter or a rebel, and of seeing at once broken the closest and most approved bonds of intimacy and friendship. He had so entire a confidence in his own intellectual superiority, and in the rights which it conferred, that he expressed it sometimes with a *näiveté* amounting almost to idolatry. One day, believing that he had won over to his ideas M. Armand Marrast, then the editor of the *National*, he wrote thus to his wife: "Marrast no longer feels any repugnance in admitting the indispensable fact of my intellectual superiority; he is in this respect, in my opinion, especially influenced by Mill, whom he holds, and with reason, in high account. To speak plainly and in general terms, I believe that, at the point at which I have now arrived, I have no occasion to do more than to continue to exist; the kind of preponderance which I covet cannot, henceforth, fail to devolve upon me."*

Shortly after the date of this letter, M. Comte was separated from his wife and embroiled with Mr. Mill himself, who had not, as the former

*Letter of the 3d December, 1842: "Auguste Comte et la philosophie positive;" p. 324.

fancied, fulfilled toward him all the duties of an accepted and loyal disciple.

I pass from the fixed idea of the man to the false idea of his system; it appears over and over again at each step in the "Cours de philosophie positive" of M. Auguste Comte,* and in the imposing biography consecrated to his memory by his most accomplished disciple, M. Littré.† I extract from different parts of these volumes the passages in which the fundamental doctrine is most clearly expressed:

"Positive philosophy is the whole body of human knowledge. Human knowledge is the result of the study of the forces belonging to matter, and of the conditions or laws governing those forces."‡

"The fundamental character of positive philosophy is, that it regards all phenomena as subjected to invariable natural laws, and con-

* Six volumes 8vo., published in the interval from 1830 to 1842 inclusive.

† Auguste Comte et la philosophie positive. 8vo. 1863.

‡ Ibid., p. 42.

siders as absolutely inaccessible to us, and as having no sense for us, every inquiry into what is termed either primary or final causes." *

"The scientific path, in which I have, ever since I began to think, continued to walk, the labors that I obstinately pursue to elevate social theories to the rank of physical science are evidently, radically, and absolutely opposed to everything that has a religious or metaphysical tendency." †

"My positive philosophy is incompatible with every theological or metaphysical philosophy, and consequently equally so with every corresponding system of policy." ‡

"M. Comte," says M. Littré, "made it a duty to speak in public without any reticence, to deduce his positive truths, and to confront them with the conceptions of Theology and of Metaphysics. . . . 'Religiosity' is in his eyes not

* Cours de philosophie positive, by M. Auguste Comte, vol. i, p. 14.

† Auguste Comte et la philosophie positive, by M. Littré, p. 194.

‡ Ibid., p. 210.

only a weakness, but an avowal of want of power."*

"The 'positive state' is that state of the mind in which it conceives that phenomena are governed by constant laws, from which prayer and adoration can demand nothing, but to which intelligence and science may address their demands; so that, by familiarizing himself with those laws more and more, and by conforming to them more and more, man acquires an ever-growing empire over nature and over himself, which empire is the sum of all civilization. The 'theological state,' on the contrary, is that state of the mind which conceives that phenomena are the results of volition, or, if the social development has arrived at Monotheism, that they are the results of a single, all-wise, and all-powerful will. This providence, essentially collective where Polytheism is supposed, essentially single in the case of Monotheism, governs the world, dispenses its good and its evil, lays its finger upon

* Auguste Comte et la phil. pos., by M. Littré, pp. 198–255.

human events, and regards the destiny of each individual man. Such is the contrast between the two doctrines. . . . Profiting by the instruction of the illustrious De Maistre, our French priests at last comprehended that ultramontanism was the only logical consequence deducible from their essential principles. The more the positive school defines the real character of its progress, the more must we see this retrograde concentration also develop itself; which will involve at some later epoch Deists themselves, as Positivism proceeds to gain complete ascendancy; an ascendancy, in other respects, far more likely to be furthered than retarded by such coordination of its adversaries, for this will tend to give at last to the struggles of philosophy a decisive character; but the Positivists will alone succeed in prevailing (at least as far as speculative doctrines are concerned) over the coalition of all the philosophical forces of the ancient school, whether metaphysical or theological." *

* Auguste Comte et la phil. pos., by M. Littré, pp. 370, 434.

M. Comte had even more aversion for Metaphysics than for Theology. He took particular offense at the contemporary spiritualistic school, and the scientific psychology of MM. Royer, Collard, Maine de Biran, Cousin, and Jouffroy. "In no view," said he, "is there any room for this illusory psychology; this final transformation of a theology, which men strive, nowadays, so idly to reanimate; for—without troubling itself either with the physiological study of our intellectual organs, or with the observation of those rational processes, which in effect direct our different scientific researches—Psychology pretends to arrive at the discovery of the fundamental laws of the human mind by contemplating that very mind—that is to say, by making complete abstraction both of causes and of effects."*

Even while absolutely rejecting Theology, M. Comte treated it with more esteem than

* Cours de philosophie positive, by M. Auguste Comte, vol. i, p. 34.

Metaphysics. "We are," he said, "too disposed, nowadays, to ignore the immense benefits due to religious influence. The positive philosophy, however paradoxical it may be to claim for it such a peculiarity, is virtually the only philosophy capable of worthily appreciating all the participation of the spirit of religion in the whole grand development of humanity. Is it not directly evident that, as by an invincible organic necessity, moral efforts have almost always to combat to some degree or other the most energetic impulses of our nature; the theological spirit was imperatively called upon to furnish to social discipline that general basis which was quite indispensable at a time when human foresight, whether of men in masses or of men as individuals, was certainly far too limited to offer any sufficient *point d'appui* to influences purely rational?"

. . . "When the positive philosophy shall have acquired that character of universality which it is still without, it will be capable of replacing entirely, with all its native superiority, that theological philosophy and that metaphysical philosophy of which this universality is in these days the sole real peculiarity, and which, deprived of this motive for preference, will have for our successors nothing but an historical existence." *

I do not pause to notice in how many respects this language is superficial, confused, and incoherent. I only draw attention to the fundamental idea which it manifests—matter, the forces of matter, and its laws; these are the sole objects of human knowledge, the sole domain of the human mind. Aware of, and embarrassed by the objections which the idea has from the beginning of time excited, M. Littré has striven to rid himself of them by an admission, sincere no doubt, like everything that he thinks, and everything that he says, but full in its turn of confusion and incoherence. "The

* Cours de philosophie positive, by M. Comte, vol. v, p. 73; vol. i, p. 23.

positive philosophy," says he, "is at once a system which comprehends all that is known of the world of man and of society, and also a general method, containing in itself all the ways by which men have come to learn all these things. What is beyond, whether, materially speaking, that space without limit, or intellectually that concatenation of never-ending causes, all this is absolutely inaccessible to the human mind. By inaccessible is not meant null or non-existent. Immensity in matter, as in intellect, is connected by a close band with what we know, and it is only by such an alliance that it becomes an idea positive in itself, and of the same order; what I mean is, that by so touching and bordering what we know, immensity appears under the double character of reality and of inaccessibility. It is an ocean which dashes upon our shores, and for which we have nor bark nor sail, but the clear vision of which is as salutary as it is formidable." *

* Auguste Comte et la phil. pos., by M. Littré, p. 519.

The vision so admitted by M. Littré is not clear, and neither is it salutary; but vague, and without result. The imagery does not destroy the system which it seeks to vail from us. Every religious belief, every spiritual doctrine, God and the human soul, are discarded by Positivism, and treated as arbitrary and transitory hypotheses, which, however they may have conduced to the development of humanity, ought now to be rejected by human reason, just as the foot may throw down the ladder which has enabled it to mount to the summit. To call things by their proper names, Positivism is Materialism and Atheism, with more or less explicitness, confidently or hesitatingly, accepted as the last term of human science, and when hard pressed, taking refuge in the darkness of skepticism.

What are the foundations upon which Positivism rests? What facts, what proofs, does M. Auguste Comte adduce in support of his principles, that matter, its forces, and its laws, constitute the sole object of human knowledge, the sole domain of the human mind?

He appeals to two arguments—the one metaphysical, the other historical; the one derived from the mind of man itself, the other from the history of humanity.

I cannot here follow M. Comte in his long and complex explanation of the two orders of proofs to which he appeals in support of his system; what I shall say will, I think, suffice to demonstrate that neither can stand any serious examination.

As a metaphysician—for metaphysician he must permit himself to be called, since he makes use of metaphysics, whatever his antipathy for philosophers who bear that name;—as metaphysician, I repeat, M. Auguste Comte belongs to the sensualistic school. He thinks with Locke and Condillac, that man deduces all his ideas and all his knowledge from impressions received by him from the outer world, and from the reflections which he makes upon those impressions. He takes, therefore, as his starting point, the maxim of that school which proclaims that "there is nothing in the intelligence which has not first been in the sense." Nevertheless, whether by an act of proper and remarkable sagacity, or struck by the reply of Leibnitz, "unless the intelligence itself," he admits that sensation does not account for all that passes and develops itself in the mind of the observer of the external world. "If," he says, "on the one side every positive theory must necessarily be founded upon observation, it is, on the other side, equally plain that to apply itself to the task of observation, our mind has need of some 'theory.' If, in contemplating the phenomena, we do not immediately attach them to certain principles, not only would it be impossible for us to combine these isolated observations, so as to draw any fruit therefrom; but we should be entirely incapable of retaining them, and in most cases the facts would remain before our eyes unnoticed. The need at all times of some 'theory' whereby to associate facts, combined with the evident impossibility of the human mind at its origin forming 'theories' out of observations, is a fact which it is impossible to ignore."*

This fact, thus proved by M. Comte himself; this necessary part of the human mind, indispensable to enable it to acquire knowledge of the external world; this "theory," anterior to all observation, which man requires for the purpose himself of observing, what are they else than those universal and necessary principles proclaimed by the spiritualistic school, and to which I recently referred?—principles inherent in the human mind, which it applies as from its own stores in taking cognizance of the external world, and by virtue of which, just as one mounts a river up to its source, man mounts and mounts up to God, and up to the relations of man with God.

* Cours de philosophie positive, par M. Auguste Comte, vol. i. p. 8.

But, admitting the same fact, M. Comte does not explain it in this way. This "theory;" these principles anterior to external observation, and which the mind absolutely requires in order to be able to observe, are, according to him, pure inventions of the human mind itself, temporary instruments which the mind creates and employs in its labors until it can obtain better. "Between," says he, "two difficulties, pressed on the one hand by the necessity of observing in order to form 'theories,' and on the other by the no less imperious necessity of creating 'theories' in order to be able to deliver itself up to a series of coherent observations, the human mind at its birth would find itself shut in by a vicious circle from which it would never have had any means of escaping, had it not succeeded in opening a natural issue by the spontaneous development of theological conceptions, which presented a point to which his efforts might be concentrated, and which might furnish aliment for his activity. It is, in effect, very remarkable, that questions the most radically inaccessible to our capacities, the intimate nature of being, the origin and the end of all phenomena, should be precisely those which the intelligence propounds to itself, as of paramount importance in that primitive condition, all the other problems really admitting of solution being almost regarded as unworthy of serious meditation. The reason of this it is not difficult to discover, for experience alone could have given us the measure of our strength; and if man had not begun by entertaining an exaggerated opinion of that strength, it would never have been capable of acquiring all the development of which it is susceptible. So much does our organization exact." *

Strange error of a man, whose supreme pretension it is to found all human knowledge upon the observation of facts! At his very first step, at the first difficulty which he

* Cours de philosophie positive, par M. Auguste Comte, vol. i, pp. 9, 10.

encounters, M. Comte observes inexactly and incompletely, does not see in the facts all that the facts contain, and only explains them by assigning to the human mind, in its primitive and spontaneous operations, a hypothesis, the hypothesis of "theological conceptions." God, and man's relations with God, is a human invention, destined to support man at the commencement of his career as an intelligent being, and to occupy provisionally the place of science!

The source of this misapprehension, the capital error of Positivism in its metaphysical argument, is, that it ignores the nature and the limits of science.

The famous "enthymême" of Descartes, "I think, therefore I am," is a pleonasm. As soon as the human being says to itself "I," the human being affirms its own existence, and distinguishes itself from that external world whence it derives impressions of which it is not the author. In this primary fact are revealed the two primary objects of human knowledge:

on the one side the human being himself, the individual person that feels and perceives, that feels himself and perceives himself; on the other side, the external world that is felt and perceived: the subject and the object, (the *moi* and the *non-moi.*) Such is the twofold field, at the beginning of his intellectual existence, opened to the knowing faculty of man.

In each of these fields, whether the human being makes himself or whether he makes the external world the object of his contemplation, he proceeds by the same method; he considers particular facts, classes these under more general facts which serve as their summary, and recognizes laws that govern them, these laws being themselves facts. When this method of observation and of generalization is applied to the outer world, understanding by that world the human body also, it gives birth to the sciences of physics and of physiology. When such method is applied to the human being, regarded as distinct from the body in which he lives and by which he acts, it gives birth to the science of psychology, logic, and morals. It is not here my intention to propose a classification of the sciences, but only to determine the domain of science properly so called—that is to say, the field in which the human mind by observation gets directly at facts and at the laws of facts.

Philosophers, in their study of man and of the world, do not sufficiently consult language, the general language, the common language, that instinctive expression of the activity of the human mind. I interrogate our native language upon the question which now occupies me, and I find it reflecting the greatest light. It has, to express the results of the intellectual process which takes place in man, when regarded as the spectator of the universe and of himself, many different words: "connaître," "savoir," "croire," "connaissance," "science," "croyance," "foi." These are not mere different names to express the same idea and the same fact, they are signs of different facts and of diverse states of the human soul. If we interrogate the languages of civilized nations, ancient or modern, we find in all of them, with more or less abundance, precision or subtilty, a similar variety of terms corresponding to a similar diversity of facts.

Talleyrand said once in the chamber of Peers, "There is somebody who has more intellect than Napoleon, more intellect than Voltaire; that somebody is the Public." I also say, there is a more profound observer than Bacon, a greater philosopher than Kant; it is mankind. Mankind is right when it distinguishes in its languages knowledge from science and from belief, science from belief and from faith. Bossuet wrote a book entitled "De la Connaissance de Dieu et de soi-même;" the idea would never have occurred to him of entitling it "De la science de Dieu et de soi-même;" it would have shocked his good sense as much as his piety. The child believes the smile and the speech of its mother; in its belief there is certainly no scientific appreciation (no science) of the relations which unite it to its mother, and of the reasons which make it believe in her. Knowledge, science, belief, and faith, are facts essentially distinct, although all equally natural to the human soul; and it is impossible to confound them, to take one for the other, to annul one in favor of the other, or to attempt to reduce them to one term, without ignoring realities, and falling into enormous errors.

Such has been the constant error of M. Auguste Comte, and such is the radical vice of Positivism. M. Comte ignores the natural and permanent diversity in the intellectual states through which a man may pass in his ardent pursuit of truth. He refuses here to recognize any state as legitimate and definitive except the scientific state. He regards intuitive knowledge and instinctive belief as preparatory and transitory states, states without any rational authority; as, in short, simple steps on the way to that scientific state which alone sets man in possession of the truth. Positivism is thus led to extend the pretensions of science beyond its proper domain, that is, beyond the finite world, its facts and its laws; and as science finds itself incapable of observing and of defining infinity, Positivism is, perforce, reduced either to deny infinity, or to declare infinity absolutely inaccessible to the human mind, and so to pass it over in silence.

This negation discovers another immense error of the school and of its chief. Convinced, and with reason, that the observation of facts is the natural and constant process of the human understanding in its labor after knowledge, M. Auguste Comte has ill understood, and incompletely understood, the results of this labor. He failed to perceive that it was observation itself, carried on and accomplished by the process, no less natural and no less legitimate, of induction, which was revealing to the mind its peculiar facts and its peculiar laws, as well as the facts and the laws of the external world, within which that mind is placed. M. Comte ended by ignoring or denying the elements *à priori* of human knowledge; that is to say, the universal and necessary principles by which man raises himself to God, and has relations with God. Thus M. Comte mutilates the human mind, because he fails to observe it and to recognize it in its entirety.

He is impelled by his system to another and still more serious mutilation of human nature. After having declared matter, its forces and its laws, to be the single object of human knowledge, and these laws to be inherent in matter, eternal and invariable, what is to be said of human liberty? What place is to be assigned to human liberty in this world, in which it is powerless to create anything or to change anything, and in which there exists no power from which it can demand anything or obtain anything? Evidently, in such a system human liberty is a chimera, an idle luxury of human nature; man, with all his faculties, has nothing to do but to study matter carefully, its forces and its laws, to adapt himself to them, and to make the best use he can of them, with a view to his welfare and to the satisfaction of his desires. Fatalism is the law of man as of the world within which he lives!

The moral instincts, and the naturally lofty mind of M. Comte revolted at this consequence, although it flowed imperiously from his system. The respect which he felt for the method of observation, and for the facts which it attains to, did not permit him absolutely to ignore or expressly to deny the psychological fact of man's liberty. Sometimes he attempts to find it a place in that sum of external facts and fixed laws which is, in his opinion, the sole field for man's activity and for man's science. But such is the want of coherence of idea, that M. Comte is visibly embarrassed; consequently, in his works—more especially in his "Cours de philosophie positive,"—the most solid and consistent of all his writings in its fundamental principles—he sets almost completely aside the essential fact of human liberty, and of free will in the individual man; and in those books in which he treats of social organization, when he finds himself face to face with the wants and the rights of political liberty, that natural consequence of individual free will and of the responsibility attaching to it, he struggles to elude questions of this kind, feeling the impossibility of reconciling the principle of moral order with the despotism and the fatalism of the material world; and when he explains his views as to the government of human societies, it is easy to see that, although writing "I am, head and heart Republican,"* he is, in his dreams, rather substituting a scientific domination for a theocratic domination than instituting any liberal *régime.*

After metaphysics comes history. M. Comte appeals to the annals of all nations and all ages

* Auguste Comte et la phil. pos., by M. Littré, p. 251.

in confirmation of his system of the world and of humanity. This history is to be divided, according to him, into three successive states, the theological state, the metaphysical state, and the scientific state. In the theological state and epoch, the human mind and social institutions are under the empire of pretended supernatural powers, of several such or of only one such, invented by man for the solution of the natural problems which lay siege to man, and for the determination of the laws, with which the social order cannot dispense. In the metaphysical epoch and state, vain abstractions essay to replace the supernatural powers of the theological state, and only end in an anarchy, both of opinions and society. The third epoch is destined to be the reign of positive science, founded solely upon observation and respect for the facts, the forces, and the laws of that external world which is the theater of man's existence. The first two states are, according to him, essentially irrational and transitory. They are the first steps of that which M. Comte styles the grand evolution of humanity, of which the *régime* of science is the end and the summit.

It would be difficult more entirely to deform, difficult to show greater ignorance of man's general history. That which M. Comte regards as three successive states in the history of the human race is only the complex and permanent condition of humanity, agitated by movements swaying in different directions, according as it meets with the successes or encounters the reverses, the hopes, or the fears to which different nations and generations are subject. That theological conceptions and metaphysical meditations are only transitory facts, "which," according to the expression of M. Comte, "will have henceforth only an historical existence," is an assertion no more true of such facts than of those that the study of physics supplies. These different yearnings of the mind, and their different labors, are the very essence—the indestructible and indivisible essence—of human nature. At no time and in no country have men more ceased, or will they more cease, to pray to God, and to strive to comprehend him, than they will cease to study the physical world, and to make it subserve their interests. Nations and generations of individuals, in different ages, have advanced more or less in one or other of these careers of intellectual activity; and so they will continue to advance. Religious faith, metaphysical meditation, and scientific inquiry have their alternations of enthusiasm and of languor, of glory and of sterility; they appear and they prosper, sometimes separately, sometimes simultaneously. If India plunged herself deep among the symbols of mythology and amid the void of Pantheism, Greece cultivated with like success the metaphysical and the natural sciences—Aristotle was the contemporary of Plato. Where other nations fluctuated variously between theological conceptions, metaphysical abstractions, and scientific studies, the Hebrew people continued, in the theological state, Monotheists. In the sixteenth century, when the spirit of free inquiry and of independence was awakened, and made its influence felt far and wide, Christian faith, at the same time, was resuscitated and confirmed; and the eighteenth century founded at once the political liberty of Protestant England and the philosophical and literary glory of Catholic France. The human mind has, according to time and place, its favorite labors and its favorite impulses; but it subsists always one and entire; it never renounces any one of its grand hopes or of its grand operations; and those men strangely mutilate and debase it who represent the mind as having, during ages, lost itself in the vain effort to attain a knowledge of God and of its own nature, and who condemn it henceforth to take up its quarters in the science of matter—of its forces—of its laws.

Why need I appeal to history for a proof of the simultaneous and indestructible co-existence of these different conditions of humanity, among which M. Auguste Comte refuses to admit more than one as rational and definitive? M. Comte has himself undertaken—he alone—to furnish me with this proof. This intractable adversary of all religious belief and tendency could not, even for the short space of this life, himself remain indifferent to such belief and tendency; during this brief period he traversed, and in the inverse order of his own theories, each of the different intellectual states which he had assigned as the successive stages of the human race. He had placed the theological state at the beginning and the scientific state at the close of the career of humanity; after having made his own *début* by the scientific state, it was as impossible for him, as it is for the human race, to content himself with that, and he himself ended there, where, according to him, mankind had commenced, namely, with the theological state. He had declared his positive philosophy to be "in radical and absolute contradiction to every kind of religious or metaphysical tendency." He had separated with *éclat* from the Saint-Simonians, "for they will soon," he said, "sink themselves in ridicule and contempt. Only imagine, their heads are turned to such a degree, that they propose nothing less than the establishment of a real, new religion, a sort of incarnation of the divinity in the person of Saint-Simon."* And some years after holding this language, and while still in the plenitude of bodily vigor and thought, M. Comte in his turn launched into a theological career; he took it upon him to transform Positivism into a religion. By the most violent of all personified abstractions, he made out of humanity the great being, the real being, sovereign and adorable, and he placed that being in the place of God, declaring himself at the same time to be his chief priest. He had more than once proclaimed that all religion was

*Letter of the 9th December, 1828, to M. Gustave d'Eichthal. Auguste Comte et la philosophie positive, by M. Littré, p. 173.

essentially founded upon the supernatural; and yet a religion all natural—the religion of humanity, the worship of humanity, the church of humanity, were summoned by him to succeed to the Christian religion and to the Church of Christ. On the 19th of October, 1851, when terminating his third philosophical course on the general histories of humanity, M. Comte summed it up in these words: "In the name of the past and of the future, the theoretical servitors and the practical servitors of humanity are about to assume worthily the direction of the general affairs of this world, in order to construct, at last, the true providence, moral, intellectual, and material, at the same time excluding irrevocably from political supremacy all the different slaves of God—Catholics, Protestants, or Deists—as being at once in arrear of the age and its perturbators." The positivist religion thus proclaimed, a positivist catechism and a positivist calendar—these last both composed by M. Comte—reduced his principles to practice.

In a series of conversations between "The Priest and the Woman," the catechism first establishes and explains the dogma, then the worship, of the new religion, its internal order and its external order, its private worship and its public worship. And the calendar, by a retrospective chronology, determines for any given year of thirteen months, and for the seven days of the week, the names of the grand servitors in every department of humanity, who are to replace the Christian saints: three hundred and sixty-four names, men and women, with one hundred and sixty-five additional names, are inscribed upon this list, which begins with Moses and ends with Bichat, passing through Homer, Aristotle, Archimedes, Cæsar, Saint Paul, Charlemagne, Dante, Gutenburg, Shakspeare, Descartes, and Frederic the Second!

A chaos is a sorry sight; a chaos of the soul a still sorrier spectacle than a chaos of worlds! Epochs of moral and social crises, even while they bring on and prepare for mankind eras of mighty progress, throw also great and potent intellects into chaos. Under the seduction of a noble ambition, and the delusion of a partial success, they enthusiastically attach themselves to some special subject, some incomplete idea; vain of their shallow and confused systems, or rather of the brilliant coloring in which they invest them, they pretend to explain and regulate man and the world, and yet are nothing more than their superficial and presumptuous observers. Among these "great lost ones of humanity," (I borrow a phrase of their own,) M. Comte was one of the most disinterested and the most sincere. The sincerity and the courage evinced by him in expressing his convictions led him on from inconsequence to inconsequence; in his benighted course he caught glimpses occasionally of grand ideas, and of these he apprehended neither the scope nor the connection: first it was an idea of a science excluding all idea of religion; and then a certain idea of a religion reconciled with and intimately united with the idea of science; turn by turn he gave himself up to the one and to the other with a blind and a daring devotedness. Had he appeared in Greece at the great era of philosophy, or in France in the seventeenth century, in the midst of the great Christian controversy, he would have been taxed with insanity—at the one epoch, not only by Plato but by Aristotle; at the other, not only by Bossuet but by Spinoza. In our days he has been more fortunate: he attached himself passionately to the method of observation of facts, which is the very character of science, and although his observations were superficial, inexact, and incomplete—although he fell into the strangest inconsistencies—the fundamental principle of his system, and the coincidence of his primary ideas with the method and the tendency of the physical sciences, the darling study of our age, have given him more importance and more influence than were really his due.

FIFTH MEDITATION.

PANTHEISM.

No two essays at philosophy are more dissimilar—I should indeed say more contradictory—than Pantheism and Positivism. What Positivism declares to be impossible, Pantheism seeks to accomplish; what Positivism forbids man to seek, Pantheism promises to give him. It is the fundamental principle of Positivism to confine the human mind to the finite world, its facts and its laws; Pantheism aspires at a knowledge and a comprehension of Infinity, and of the relations of the finite with Infinity. "I have explained God, God's nature and his attributes," says Spinoza.*

* Ethics, 1st part; of God: Appendix, vol. i, p. 39. French translation by M. Saisset.

I hasten to explain, in order to prevent misconstruction; it is to Pantheism, properly so called—to the sole system that merits the name—that my remarks are here applicable. "We must," says M. Cousin, "it seems, distinguish two kinds of Pantheism. The assertion that this visible universe, indefinite or infinite, suffices to itself, and that there is nothing to be sought for beyond, is the Pantheism of Diderot, Helvetius, de la Mettrie, d'Holbach. This Pantheism is clearly Atheism, and it would not be very easy to comprehend the complacent indulgence that should spare it that name of Atheism—a name, unfortunately, of ancient date, which would then have no longer any object to fit it, and would need to be erased from our dictionary. But is it possible for a similar Pantheism to be imputed to Spinoza? With the French Encyclopedists, things exist in particularity and individuals singly: the universe is an assemblage of individuals—an assemblage without unity, or of which the sole unity is a presumed primary matter, which the philosopher admits or which he does not admit, but with which his thought has no business to occupy itself. With Spinoza, on the contrary, the single substance is all, and the individuals are nothing. This substance is not the nominal unity of the assemblage of individuals, each of which exists singly, but is the single really existing substance, and in the presence of that substance the world and man are but shadows; so that from the 'Ethics' may be gathered an exaggerated Theism which leaves no individual existing as such. Rigorously, and at bottom, there is here perhaps only one and the same system, but a system, nevertheless, with two very different forms—the one, where God is nothing but the Universe; the other, where the Universe exists only in God."*

I think, with M. Cousin, that, rigorously and at bottom, there is here but one and the same system, but in appearance, and I say besides, in

* Histoire générale de la philosophie, p. 433, ed. 1863.

the opinion of its authors, the difference is great, and requires to be noticed. I postpone for the subject "Materialism," all that I have to say upon the subject of the so-called Pantheism, which admits no other existence than either that of the individualities that people the visible universe, or that of the primary matter whence they have issued. I occupy myself, at this moment, solely with the idealistic Pantheism.

Do we wish to behold a spectacle of how weak the human mind really is in the midst of all its grandeur, and of the limits which must finally and abruptly check its progress, however high its flight, we will read Plotinus, Spinoza, and Hegel, three martyrs to intellectual ambition, differing very much according to the difference of the eras and the nations to which they respectively belong, but similar in this point at least, that they ignore the visible world, and leave it behind them, to enter that world which dazzles their sight, where they plunge into a void in quest of what they call "Being!"

Two passions have impelled, are impelling, and will, probably, still occasionally impel men of eminent powers of mind to Pantheism: the passionate craving for an universal science, and the passionate longing for universal unity—feelings noble both, but illegitimate and incapable of satisfaction.

"I have resolved," said Spinoza, "to search if there exist a real Good, a Good capable, singly, of filling the entire soul after it shall have rejected all the rest—in a word, a Good that gives the soul, when the soul finds it and possesses it, the eternal and supreme happiness. . . . Man is essentially a being that thinks, and the highest degree of human knowledge ought to be the highest degree of human felicity. . . . My sources of enjoyment consist in the exercise of the reason." *

* Œuvres de Spinoza, French translation of M. Emile Saisset, vol. i, pp. 15, 16.

What obliviousness of man's nature and of man's life! Man is not merely a being that thinks, but a being that feels, wills, and acts, a being moral and responsible for his acts, at the same time that he is a being of intelligence, and a being insatiate of knowledge. It is by his thought that he accounts to himself for his sentiments, and for the motives of his acts, but it is not from his thought that he derives either his sentiments or his liberty, neither does knowledge constitute his sole enjoyment. Spinoza mutilates man strangely when he places "the highest degree of human felicity in the highest degree of human knowledge." Man is more exacting than the philosopher, and it requires infinitely more to satisfy the most modest human soul than to satisfy the proudest mind. Infinitely more in respect of happiness, infinitely less in respect of science! Not that I would make their intellectual ambition a reproach to philosophers, even when it leads them astray. It is an honor to the human mind that it aspires higher than it can attain, that it torments itself in the struggle to carry its science into that invisible world, which it instinctively feels by anticipation, just as it does into that visible world that it sees. God granted to man this privilege; he implanted in his soul the ardent desire to know him and to possess him fully. But at the same time, God granted to men in general certain instincts and spontaneous beliefs which adequately satisfy this desire without the necessity of any profound study. What would have become of the human race if, in order to believe in God, to hope in him, and to pray to him, man had been obliged to wait until philosophers had resolved the problems which still weigh upon *their* genius? As God, in creating man free, took care that the maintenance of the general order in this world should not be completely abandoned to the disputes of men, so did he provide for the spiritual nourishment of mankind, without denying to the great ambitious ones of the earth either the prospect of a satisfaction more complete, or the right to search for it.

Let us never tire of repeating, this is the mystery of man's mixed nature—an indication of a destiny in store for him superior to his actual condition. He carries within him the ideas of infinity, of perfection, and yet here below he is nothing but a finite being, imperfect, equally incapable of sufficing to himself and of satisfying himself, either in the domain of thought or of actual life. "There are more things in heaven and upon earth than philosophy—than even the philosophy 'of the absolute' —can explain. . . . To comprehend God, it needs to be God. A child might have said as much to Hegel." These words I borrow from M. Edmond Scherer's exposition of the doctrine of Hegel.* Jesus in effect said, eighteen centuries ago: "I praise thee, Father, Lord of heaven and of earth, that thou hast hidden these things from the wise and prudent, and hast revealed them unto babes."

* Mélanges d'histoire religieuse, pp. 366, 341. 1864.

Pantheists are entirely of the opinion of M. Scherer, for to enable man to comprehend God, they have found no other expedient than to make of man himself the God that man is desirous of comprehending. The passion for an universal science has ended by receiving no being as God but man.

The passion for universal unity has led to the same result. That truth is one—that is to say, that all truths, whatever their object, are in harmony with one another—the very word truth implies and proclaims. From the unity of truth the Pantheists passed, with a single bound, to the unity of being. They identified idea and reality, science and existence, confounding all things in order to reduce them to one single thing, and abolishing all beings in order to concentrate them all in one and the same being, which, after all, is nothing more than an impersonal notion and a barren name, falling in its turn into the void.

By what path did the Pantheists arrive at

this abyss? What was the process employed by men of eminent powers of mind to construct a system so singularly factitious and hypothetical, and yet pretending, at the same time, to be so necessary and so rigorously philosophical?

Like some great men of antiquity, (and their number is considerable,) who sought to explain nature and the physical world by incomplete and precipitate hypotheses and systems, invented irrespectively of either facts or their laws, the Pantheists by similar means proceeded—nay, are proceeding—to explain man, the universe, and God; the Infinite and the finite. The method which for three centuries has constituted the glory of the natural sciences, and made their progress lasting, the exact study of facts and their relations; that method so long strange not only to general philosophy but to the special sciences themselves—I may at once call it by its proper name, the scientific method —was formerly, and remains still, strange to the Pantheists; to Spinoza as to Plotinus, to Hegel as to Spinoza. Whether Plotinus plunges into an *ecstacy* to arrive at and comprehend God in uniting man to God by the virtue of contemplation; or Spinoza, defining *substance*, makes it the principle from which to deduce his theory of the universe and of its unity; or Hegel, speaking of *idea* in order to arrive at the same result as Spinoza, seeks to obtain from his term *substance*—it is the same defect that appears in the labors of all these potent intelligences, not only in their development, but in the very point from which they start; for observation of facts and of their laws they substitute the affirmation and the definition of an axiom, and the deduction, logical, it is true, of its consequences. They disdain and set aside all study of the realities of the universe, believing themselves to be in possession of a key to open its secrets.

They see not that their key is a deception, that at each step facts evident, indestructible, give the flattest denial to their inferences, and that to maintain their arbitrary and insufficient principle they are forced to ignore and to deny other facts, themselves evident, indestructible.

Psychological observation proves and irresistibly establishes three facts, however the consequences of these facts themselves may lead to questions and controversies.

1. Man believes in his own existence, and in his own personality. He feels himself and perceives himself to be a being, real and distinct from every other being.

2. Man feels himself and knows himself to be a free agent. Of the freedom of his resolves, whatever the motives and deliberations which precede them, man has an intimate and assured consciousness.

3. Good and evil exist in man, and exist in the world; moral good and evil as well as physical good and evil. Whatever may be thought of their origin, the mixture and the struggle of good and of evil, in the moral order and in the

physical order, are facts evident in themselves, and attested by the conscience and by the experience of the human race.

Pantheism sometimes ignores and omits, sometimes formally denies, these facts, which psychology attests and proves. There is, however, a notable difference in this point in the three great representatives of Pantheism. Thanks to the Platonic school, from which he sprang, Plotinus, in treating the different questions of man's liberty and of the reality of good and of evil, soars in an elevated region where the truth now shines in splendor, now obscures itself and disappears in the labyrinth in which the philosopher himself is entangled as soon as he attempts to explain the one and infinite Being and that Being's relations with nature and with man. Spinoza is more consequent and plainer. He formally denies all individuality, all human liberty. Substance, "*the being*," is single and universal. All act of man, as every fact of nature, is produced by fated laws and causes: "Free will is a chimera, flattering to our pride and in reality founded upon our ignorance. All that I can say to those who believe that they can, by virtue of any free decision of the soul, speak or be silent—or, to use a single word, act—is that they dream with their eyes open."* . . . "Nothing," adds he, "is bad in itself. Good and evil indicate nothing positive in things considered in themselves, and are nothing but manners of thinking. Not only has every man the right to seek his good, his pleasure, but he cannot do otherwise. . . . The measure of each man's right is his power. . . . He who does not yet know reason, or who, having not as yet contracted the habit of virtue, lives according to the laws only of his appetites, is as much in his right as he who regulates his life according to the laws of reason. In other words, just as the sage has an absolute right to do all that his reason dictates to him, or to live

* Œuvres de Spinoza, French translation of M. E. Saisset, vol. i, Introduction, p. clii.

according to the laws of his reason, in the same manner has the ignorant man and the madman a right to everything that his appetite impels him to take; in other words, the right to live according to the laws of appetite. . . . And he is no more obliged to live according to the laws of good sense than a cat is obliged to live under the laws that govern the nature of a lion. . . . Hence we conclude that a compact has only a value proportioned to its utility; where the utility disappears the compact disappears too with it, and loses all its authority. There is, then, folly in pretending to bind a man forever to his word; unless, at least, man so contrive that the breach of the compact shall entail for him that violates it more danger than profit."*

Hegel is less absolute and less blind. Of a mind large, and from its greatness naturally just, he escaped at moments the yoke of his system. Struck by the particular truths, moral,

* Œuvres de Spinoza, vol. i, pp. clix, clx.

historical, æsthetic, that offered themselves to his view in the theater of the universe, he admitted them without very well knowing what place he should assign to them. "He was," said one of his most intelligent disciples, "a conciliator in his philosophy. His philosophy stands midway between Theism and Pantheism; between historical right, as the expression of actual reason, and the absolute right to liberty and equality, as the end of universal history. His system seems to sanction the most profound piety, and to regard Christianity as the true and absolute religion, at the very time when it appears also as its negation; just as in politics it presents itself as at one and the same moment conservative and progressive, favorable to existing rights and yet revolutionary."*

"It is impossible," says M. Edmond Scherer,

* Histoires de la philosophie allemande depuis Kant jusqu'a Hegel, by S. Willm: a work crowned by the Institute: vol. iv, p. 337.

'to read Hegel without asking ourselves if he, be serious. He falls incessantly into a style of images and personifications; and one would suppose one's self, in perusing his writings, to be present at the formation of a mythology, at the development of a world like that of the ancient Gnostics, in which notions assumed forms and marched on, passing through all kinds of adventures."* M. Edmond Scherer's is a mind hard to please, which is ever struck and offended by incoherence of objects, futility of artificial combinations, and vain play upon words, even where he recognizes or admires the genius. The philosophical "rout" is not embarrassed for so slight a cause; it marches straight to the object toward which the dominant idea, once adopted, gives the impulse. In spite of its complexities and of its craving for the reconciliation of religion and of politics, the Pantheism of Hegel has borne its natural fruits. A school has resulted from it, which, in accord-

* Mélanges d'histoire religieuse, pp. 298, 338.

ance with its proper and independent manifestations, a learned and moderate judge, M. Willm, characterizes in these words: "The new German philosophy, of which Feuerbach, Bruno Bauer, and Arnold Rüge are the principal chiefs, comes, in its ultimate results, in contact with the *Humanism* of M. Pierre Leroux, the *Positivism* of M. Auguste Comte, and the *Atheism* of M. Proudhon. It tends to substitute for the ancient worship the worship of humanity, and to found a new worship dispensing with God, and with morality properly so called. . . . There is no such thing as *theology* but only *anthropology;* for the mind of humanity is the divine mind realized. There is no longer any other piety than devotedness to the objects of humanity; no longer any other prayer than the contemplation of the human mind. . . . Man accomplishes every reasonable object if he accomplishes his own peculiar object, and he cannot do better than employ all his faculties to realize his own objects.

Man's will be done: such is the principle of the new law."*

Such is the inevitable result at which Pantheism, even that kind termed idealistic Pantheism, ultimately arrives, whatever the elevation of mind and the morality of intent in its first authors. This is no scientific doctrine, founded upon the observation of facts and their laws; it is an hypothesis framed by dint of violent abstractions, verbal commutations and reasoning, in the blindness of a thought drunk with itself. Under the breath of Pantheism all beings—real and personal beings—vanish, and are replaced by an abstraction becoming in its turn the Being *par excellence;* the sole being, although without personality and without volition, swallowing up all things in a bottomless abyss, which absorbs that being, too, after it has already absorbed everything that it has sought so to explain.

* Histoire de la philosophie allemande, depuis Kant jusqu'a Hegel: by S. Willm: vol. iv, pp. 624, 626.

Was there ever, in the conceptions of mythology, or in the mystical dreams of the human imagination, anything so artificial, anything so vain, as this hypothesis, which at its very beginning, as well as throughout its entire course, loses sight of the best attested facts respecting man and the world; and, shocking equally science and common sense, departs as much from the method of philosophy as from the spontaneous instincts of mankind?

SIXTH MEDITATION.

MATERIALISM.

Materialistic Pantheism is more consistent and more intelligible. I must at once restore to it its genuine name; it has no right to that of Pantheism: it sees God neither in the universe nor in man; the eternal world and ephemeral individuals are, in its eyes, only combinations and different forms of matter. It is Materialism in its principle, and Atheism in its consequences.

Two things strike me in the actual state of men's minds; the progress that Materialism is making, and its constant timidity in that very progress.

The progress of Materialism is evident; progress in the learned world and in the unlearned world, in the name of the scientific studies and of popular tendencies. A contemporary spiritualistic philosopher, as distinguished by intellectual probity as by the independence and the moderation of his opinions, of whom the Duke de Broglie, on learning his death, exclaimed, "We have lost a sage"—M. Damiron I mean—published eight years ago his "Mémoires pour servir à l'histoire de la philosophie au 18e siècle;" he had read it in successive parts to the *Académie des Sciences Morales et Politiques.* He said in his preface, "Men are disposed a second time to have Sensualism; they insist upon something that they may oppose to and substitute for pure and simple Spiritualism: be it so; but then let them at least well understand what it is that they are asking for. It is not merely Locke, the moderate chief of the school, nor is it d'Alembert, nor Saint-Lambert, nor even Helvetius; these keep themselves relatively within bounds: it is Diderot who has so little moderation, it is d'Holbach, it is

Naigeon, it is Lalande, and de la Mettrie; it is a whole order of minds, not very eminent, but very decided and very consistent and logical in their materialism; materialists in all and for all, from the soul up to God—not forgetting, be it remembered, liberty, duty, a future life, etc. . . . These men, with their heads in the air and their masks in their hand, with a confidence in themselves and a faith almost confounding itself with religion, profess openly as truth, fatalism, egotism, and atheism. This is what men want, and what, if they wish to be logical, men must want, when, closely or remotely, they adhere to a philosophy that reduces everything to sensation, and that which is the object of sensation. Let there then be no illusion upon this subject; all the principles of morals and of religion are at stake. Sensualism *is* what it is, and *can* be nothing else. It was made a complete system in the eighteenth century; nothing remains in it that can be either made or remade; and if men recur to it in our days, the mechanism and the form may be altered—for these are variable—but not the essential substance, for that is *not* so. There are not two manners of being consequent any more in this system than in any other; however the attempt may be made, men can never by any reproduction render it what it is not, and what its nature prevents it from ever being; so we must take it or we must leave it alone; we cannot change its principles.*

What M. Damiron eight years ago felt would occur, has been accomplished rapidly. Sensualism, in its true nature as Materialism, has resumed its activity and returned to the stage; now tacitly admitted by sober, studious men, now loudly professed and loudly proclaimed by the "enfants terribles" of the school; professed and proclaimed not only with all its principles, but with all its consequences.

* Mémoires pour servir à l'histoire de la philosophie au 18e siècle, by Ph. Damiron, member of the Institute; vol. i, p. xiv. 1858.

A profound sentiment of hesitation and embarrassment clings, nevertheless, to the doctrine of Materialism. The most distinguished of its adepts struggle to give explanations that look like disavowals, and many repudiate the charge of being Materialists as if it were an insult. "I have never," says M. de Remusat, "observed without astonishment the testy sensibility of philosophers upon this point. Who is there that has not witnessed the indignation manifested by the followers of the philosophy of sensation when they hear retraced to them the positive consequences of this doctrine? It seems just as if their rightful claims were being disavowed, or as if they were being denounced; as if the Inquisition were still at hand, with its tortures and its auto-da-fès; or as if their refuters were sending them to martyrdom. A general timidity reigns throughout their school; they seem to think freedom of opinions never sufficiently assured, and society never tolerant enough, for their philosophy to declare and avow itself for such as it is. Whether from shame or from fear, Materialism asks to be tenderly handled, suspects that every one who defines her has the designs of a persecutor, makes protestations of her good intentions, and is alarmed at her very faith. She defends herself from the imputation of believing only in the senses, even while making sensation the one universal fact. It might be said that she blushes at matter just as persons infirm of faith blush at the name of Jesus. Perhaps this may be an indirect proof of the distrust which their cause inspires in Materialists, and an involuntary avowal that the human mind belongs not to them."*

Whence arise, what signify, these two contradictory facts: on the one side, the perseverance and the facility with which, in our days, Materialism reproduces and propagates itself; on the other side, the uneasiness and the

* Essais de philosophie, by Charles de Remusat: vol. ii, p. 179.

timidity which it inspires in many of those even who admit it?

Materialism is the doctrine of appearances. "Specious doctrine," says M. Vacherot, "to those whose conception of things depends solely upon their ability to picture them to themselves."* It is by their material appearances that, at the outset, the external world and man himself manifest themselves to the human mind. It is only by reflection and by a process of observation within itself that it penetrates beyond mere appearances, and discovers what appearances alone would never enable it to see. To minds at once active and superficial, inquisitive, impatient to acquire science, although not very nice as to the kind, Materialism is a commodious and apparently clear solution of certain difficult and obscure questions which fasten irresistibly upon the human understanding.

Besides all this, these questions, and the

* La métaphysique et la science, vol. i, p. 171.

different solutions of which they are susceptible, have their epochs of ardor or languor, of favor or discredit. In our days, the fruitful activity and the brilliant progress of the sciences of the material world, come in aid of the doctrine of Materialism. This progress is, however, far from being as exclusive of other progress as is often said. Although less popular than a few years ago, Spiritualism has not ceased to be an active and influential doctrine in the elevated region of philosophy, and the Christian awakening persists and develops itself energetically in the face of the adversaries of Christianity. The times in which we live are entitled to more justice than men accord to them; intellectual labors are now very extensive and very varied; the most different tendencies coexist, and pursue their independent career. Even in this, Materialism is again the doctrine of appearances; it is neither so strong nor so near its triumph as it has the air of being.

Nothing proves this better than the hesitation and persistent embarrassment of the most distinguished among its adherents. The circumstance noticed by M. de Remusat twenty-five years ago, is recurring at the present day as plainly as ever. Sometimes we find disavowals of the consequences of the principle of Materialism, and attempts of all kinds to escape from those consequences; sometimes we find efforts made to disguise the principle itself under purer colors. A general and enduring instinct in man persists in protesting against the appearances upon which Materialism is founded. Man does not believe either himself or the universe to be exclusively matter. The distinction between matter and mind is a natural and spontaneous, a primitive and permanent, belief of the human race.

And is this, then, merely an instinct and an aspiration, a proud pretension of human nature? Is it not, on the contrary, the innate sentiment, the intimate knowledge of that *essential fact* in humanity of which observation recognizes and evidences the existence?

The fact to which I allude is the following: As soon as a consciousness of life is awakened in man—as soon as he feels and perceives what is taking place within him—he has a perception of himself as of a real, personal, and distinct being. He gives voice to this feeling and this perception as soon as he uses the word "I," and he does so before he has any clear knowledge in detail of the being whose existence he so recognizes and affirms.

When, in the natural development of life, man thus makes himself as a real and personal being, the object of his own observation, he recognizes in himself as such real and personal being certain facts in their nature essentially different. On the one side, he recognizes a body inherent in his being, which forms part of his being, and through which he communicates with the external world, either by the impressions which he receives from that world, or by the modes in which he acts upon that world. On the other side, whether he regard himself as, so to say, the theater of action, or as the very actor, he recognizes himself to be a single being, a being permanent and abiding, ever the same in the midst of the variety of his personal impressions or of his actions upon the world beyond him; and this, too, in spite of the complications and incessant transformations of his body, the organ and the medium of those impressions and actions.

Thus it is that in man's consciousness there is a manifestation and proof at once of the unity and of the complex nature of the human being; that is, in accordance with the spontaneous language of mankind, at once of the distinction and of the union of the soul and of the body. This is the primitive and essential fact of man in his actual life.

In proportion as the human being develops himself, as he extends the circle of his observations upon the world and upon himself, special facts confirm the general truth of which I have just given a summary, and prove the essential distinction of the soul and the body by the essential diversity of the properties of each. Thus the body, in its organization and in its life, is subject to fixed and pre-established laws, over which man's will has no control or power; whereas the soul is essentially free, and capable of determining itself and of acting from motives foreign to the laws which govern the body. Fatality is the condition of the human being in corporeal existence; liberty is his privilege in his moral life. I say in his moral life, and the expression reveals between the soul and the body another essential and ineffaceable difference. The body is strange to every idea of morality, abandoned to the exigencies of its necessities and its appetites; it has no aspiration, no tendency but to satisfy them. The soul has needs and desires of quite a different kind, and they are often contrary to those of the body; and however often the soul may yield to the tendencies of the body, not seldom also does it withstand and surmount them; and this both in persons of obscure condition, and in those who stand in the public gaze of men. When the body is dominant in man, man tends toward Materialism; when he listens to the aspirations of soul it is, on the contrary, to Spiritualism that his nature rises. The complexity of his nature manifests itself in the development of his life as in the first instinct of his consciousness; at whatever epoch he is the subject either of his own or of our observation he cannot be called exclusively body, matter, without facts giving his assertion at each step the flattest contradiction.

Whence comes this essential and primordial fact—the fact of the complexity and yet unity of the human being? How is this union of soul and body accomplished? their mutual influences exercised, how? Here, according to religion, is the mystery; here, for philosophy, lies the problem.

Materialism is but an hypothesis adopted for the explanation of this great fact, and the hypothesis consists not in the solution of the problem, but in its suppression by the denial of the fact itself. What need, they say, to seek to explain how the union of soul and body is accomplished? Neither this complexity of the human being nor his unity in that complexity is a reality. Man is only a product and an ephemeral form of matter!

I shall not refuse myself the pleasure of refuting this hypothesis by the mouth of a contemporary philosopher, whom I shall soon myself have to combat. "Nothing," says M. Vacherot, "proves that the hypothesis of Materialism is true; on the contrary, positive facts evidence its falsity. . . . If the soul be only the result of the play of the organs, how is it that the soul is able to resist the impressions and the appetites of the body, to direct, concentrate, and govern its faculties? If the will be but the instinct in a different form, how explain its empire over the instinct? This fact is an irresistible argument; it is the rock upon which Materialism has always wrecked itself, and upon which it will continue to do so. . . . The wisdom of the ancients pronounced its decree more than two thousand years ago. 'Do we not see,' says Socrates, according to Plato, 'that the soul governs all the elements of which it is pretended that it is composed? that the soul resists them throughout the whole course of life, and subdues them in every way, repressing some harshly and painfully, as where the gymnastic or the medical method is resorted to; repressing others more gently, rebuking these, warning those, speaking to desires, to anger, to fear, as to things of a nature alien to its own? So Homer, in the "Odyssey," represents Ulysses as

> "Smiting his breast, and chiding thus his heart:
> Bear this, O heart, thou that hast worse endured."*

* Στῆθος δὲ πληξὰς, κραδίην ἠνίπαπε μύθῳ,
Τέτλαθι δὲ, κραδίη. καὶ κύντερον ἄλλο ποτ' ἔτλης.
Odyssey, Book xx, v. 17.

"'Do you think,' adds Socrates, 'that Homer would have so expressed himself had, in his conception, the soul been a mere harmony, necessarily governed by the passions of the body? Did he not rather think that the soul ought to govern and master those passions, and that the soul is something far more divine than any harmony?'" *

Materialists themselves have felt the feebleness of their hypothesis; to support it they have invented a second hypothesis. "No force without matter, no matter without force," † says Dr. Buchner, at the present day one of the most resolute interpreters of the doctrine. That is to say, not being able to explain facts by matter alone, as matter is observed and conceived naturally by the human mind, they endow matter with what they term *force*, a principle of movement and of production. "Matter and

* La Métaphysique et la science, by M. Vacherot, vol. i, p. 174; Plato, Phæd. xliii.

† Le Materialisme contemporain en Allemagne, by M. Paul Janet, of the Institute, p. 20. 1864.

force are," it is now said, "inseparable; both have existed from all eternity." Thus, imperiously urged by instinct and by their observation of facts, they begin again by distinguishing and naming separately matter and force; then, all at once, they confound them, treat them as united in their essence and from all eternity, and conclude by believing that they have succeeded in giving an explanation of man and of the world!

In this, what do they more than add an abstraction to an abstraction, and an hypothesis to an hypothesis? We are here in the presence of facts that are certain and yet perplexing; in presence of an external world, which evidently has not always been such as it is, which had a beginning, which is continuing to develop itself according to certain laws, and which is tending to certain ends; in the presence, too, of man, evidently a being at once one and complex, identical and yet variable. The ancients gave names and explanations to those incontestible facts, but the names and explanations are now rejected! Still, names and explanations are needed; man must put something in the place of God, Creator, and Providence—in the place of mind, and matter, and soul, and body. It is not for the first time that man finds himself confronted by this necessity, or that he essays to satisfy it; many abstractions, many words, have been already employed for this purpose. *God* was replaced by *nature*, by *substance*, by *cause;* the *human soul* was transformed into *vital principle;* the vital principle was elevated to the dignity of soul. It seems that these words, these abstractions, have had their time and lost their credit; and so now it is *force* which replaces *them; force* is mind, *force* is soul, *force* creates, *force* is God. It is enough now that they incorporate force with body; the problem no longer exists; man and the universe are laid bare!

When Leibnitz, to combat the Idealism of Descartes, and the Pantheism of Spinoza, developed the idea of force, he did not foresee that that very notion would be one day made use of to reduce to nonentities God, the human soul, all real and personal being, all first and final cause; to reduce, in short, everything to a medley of mechanics and dynamics incarnate in matter!

However specious it may appear to superficial minds, or to minds prejudiced in its favor by the peculiar nature of their studies and of their habitual labors, Materialism, like Pantheism, is only an hypothesis—an hypothesis constructed by dint of mere abstractions and purely verbal assertions. These not only disregard or suppress the facts which they pretend to explain, but are in direct contradiction with facts themselves recognized and proved by psychological observation. It is, in effect, an hypothesis, (I am forced here to repeat what I before affirmed of Pantheism,) equally revolting to true science and to common sense.

The hypothesis of Materialism has but a

single merit; it is more consistent than those of the other systems. But even to this merit Materialism loses its title whenever it shrinks from pushing its principles boldly to their consequences, whether philosophical or practical: that is to say, whenever it shrinks from denying man's liberty, a moral law, the necessary principles of the human mind—whenever, in short, it shrinks from proclaiming its ultimate results, which are, as M. Damiron puts them, Fatalism, Egotism, Atheism. Philosophers are right in seeking for truth and in respecting truth for itself and at every risk; but there are some consequences which are the clearest evidence of a vice in principle; and this vice, in Materialism, is the blind forgetfulness of the best proved facts and the most essential elements of human nature.

SEVENTH MEDITATION.

SKEPTICISM.

There are two kinds of Skepticism, experimental Skepticism and systematic Skepticism. Experimental Skepticism is the result of the incertitude which arises in men's minds from the spectacle of the infinite variety, discordance, and mobility of human opinions. Systematic Skepticism, on the other hand, challenges the power itself of the human understanding, and declares it incapable of knowing things in their essence —reality in itself. The one is doubt applied in practice; the other is doubt affirmed as a principle.

In an essay on Skepticism, written in 1830, M. Jouffroy treated experimental and practical skepticism with great contempt: this skepticism "founds itself," says he, "only upon the apparent contradictions of human judgment. To prove that there is a contradiction either between the results at which each faculty of the mind when taken separately arrives, or between the final results attained by different faculties, as by the sense and by the reason; to establish that there is a contradiction of a like nature between the opinions received by different men or by different nations, or between those opinions themselves, which, at different epochs, have variously for a time contented humanity; then to conclude from all this that the human intelligence regards in turn as true things which are contradictory, and that consequently there is for that intelligence no truth at all: such is all the mechanism in which this second-rate skepticism consists which has fascinated, and still continues to fascinate, whole hosts of little minds. Long ago this skepticism was refuted, and at all its points; long ago the unity of human truth was demonstrated, after having been admitted *à priori* in all ages by their leading minds. This kind of skepticism is a theme upon which men will long continue to dilate; the darling subject for wits, it merits not to arrest the attention of philosophers."

By way of amends, however, for these remarks, M. Jouffroy makes an immense concession to the systematic skepticism which declares the human mind incapable of knowing things as they really are in themselves, for he admits this skepticism to be rationally legitimate; "the foundation of all belief," says he, "is an act of faith, blind but irresistible. In effect there is no contradiction between faith and skepticism; for man believes by instinct and doubts by reason. . . . Skeptics fall into no contradiction when, in the practice of life, they believe their senses, their consciousness, their memory, and when they act in consequence; they obey the laws of their instinctive nature by so believing, and they obey their rational natures by confessing that their beliefs are illegitimate.

So we equally excuse humanity which believes, and skepticism which doubts; but we cannot equally excuse the philosophers who have combated skepticism by striving to demonstrate the rational legitimacy of human belief. When men affirm that mankind believes, and that skeptics do so with mankind, they affirm a fact in itself incontestable; when they add that mankind believes itself right in believing, that is to say, virtually admits that the human intelligence sees things as they are, this is true too, and skeptics do not deny it; but when, grappling with skepticism itself, men pretend to show that the human intelligence really sees things as they are, this is a pretension which I cannot understand. What! do they not perceive that this pretension is nothing less than the pretension of demonstrating the human intelligence by the human intelligence, which has been, is, and will be eternally impossible? We believe skepticism forever invincible, because we regard skepticism as the final word of the reason concerning the reason itself." *

I do not agree with M. Jouffroy in his disdain for experimental and practical skepticism. This is not, it is true, a system which philosophers are called upon to refute, but a fact which ought to occupy an important place with them, for by showing to us how incomplete human science is, and human error how frequent, it sets us on our guard against all presumptuous confidence in our own ideas, and against intolerance toward the ideas of others —two of the most dangerous infirmities to which human intelligence and society are liable. But as for the reasoning which impels M. Jouffroy to accept the systematic and definitive skepticism as to the intrinsic reality of things, I repudiate it altogether. If that were, as he says, "the final word of the reason respecting the reason itself," it would be the negation, or to use a better expression, the

* Mélanges philosophique, pp. 238-240.

suicide, of man's reason and of the human intelligence.

In his discourse which he pronounced in 1813, on resuming his functions at the "Faculté des Lettres," M. Royer-Collard summed up his conclusions upon this fundamental question—conclusions very different, more different essentially than even apparently they are, from those arrived at by M. Jouffroy. Whereas M. Jouffroy believes systematic skepticism forever invincible, "because he regards it as the final word of the reason concerning the reason," M. Royer-Collard, on the contrary, ends his discourse with these words: "We cannot divide man; we cannot assign a part only to skepticism; as soon as skepticism once penetrates into the understanding, it invades it throughout." I would confirm this conclusion of M. Royer-Collard, by carrying still further the reasoning which led him to it.

"The most general result," says he, "presented by the history of modern philosophy—

its most striking characteristic when contrasted with ancient philosophy—is its skepticism with respect to the existence of the external world; that world in which mankind has so long believed, which begins to reveal itself in us with our existence itself, and in the bosom of which we are forced to perceive ourselves as mere fragments of its immensity. . . . I am not here to reason in favor of the received opinion; that opinion needs neither proofs nor defenders; it is rooted deeply enough in our most intimate nature to brave all attack. It is not the world that risks anything at the hands of the philosophers; it is rather the honor of philosophy which suffers some discredit; it is rather philosophy that relieves the vulgar from a part of the respect which philosophy yet demands at its hands, when it gives birth to paradoxes bearing, seemingly, the very impress of folly. Moreover, whether the material world really exist or not, is not a matter in controversy; this question would resolve itself into one still more general—whether all those faculties of ours, of which the authority is indivisible, are organs of truth or organs of falsehood; and upon this point we shall ever be driven to accept the testimony of those very organs. The sole question which belongs to philosophical analysis, consists in examining if it be certain that our faculties attest to us the existence of an external world, and if the human race believes in this existence; for if it believes in it, this universal belief becomes a fact in our intellectual constitution; and whether this fact be a primitive one, or a deduction from any anterior fact—whether it be the immediate teaching of nature or an acquisition by reasoning—it is entitled to its place unmutilated in the synthetic table of science. Has it disappeared? Then the man of philosophy is not the man of nature; science is false, and consequently, the analysis without fidelity; and one may rest assured that philosophers have inserted in the understanding some principle, or some fact, which was not there before; or that they have not collected with care all the principles and facts which are actually there."

Having thus formalized the question, M. Royer-Collard follows it up with an inquiry as exact as it is profound, of the psychological fact of the perception of the external world which accompanies the fact of sensation: this inquiry leads him to this conclusion:

"Sensation has no object; sensation is merely relative to the sentient being; if not perceived, sensation does not exist. But the perception, which affirms an external existence, supposes two things—the mind which perceives, and the object which is perceived; the being that thinks, and the being that is the subject-matter of thought. Just as the sensation is relative to the mind, so is the act of the perception relative to it also, and just so does it suppose the mind; the object, on the contrary, supposes neither the mind nor the mind's perception. The object does not exist because we perceive it; but we perceive it because it exists—because we are endowed with the faculty of perception. In a city inhabited no longer, there remain no sensation, no idea, no judgment; the houses remain, and even the streets, and with them nature, with all nature's laws, which are not suspended in their course. To the universe, the energetic presence of its Creator suffices; it does not require our presence; the absence of spectators would not make it languish; it existed before us, it will exist after us; its reality is independent of us and of our thoughts—it is absolute. The authority which persuades us of this is no less than that of the consciousness itself; it is the authority of the primitive laws of thought, and to man's mind those laws are absolute laws of truth. The same draught may convey the impression of sweetness and of bitterness, because sensation is relative to the variable state of sensibility, and sensibility itself is relative to organization; but the laws of the mind are an immutable standard. The imperfection of knowledge does not render it uncertain, and although it admits of degrees, it does not admit of contradiction. Our limited faculties do not, it is true, perceive all that there is in things; but still, what they do perceive, is in effect there just as they perceive it. . . . If a man call upon me to prove this by reasoning, I shall, in my turn, demand of him, too, that he first prove to me by reasoning that reasoning is more convincing than perception; that he at least prove that the memory, without which there is no such thing as reasoning, is a faculty more to be relied upon than those faculties whose testimony they reject.

Intellectual life is an uninterrupted succession, not merely of ideas, but of beliefs, explicit or implicit. The beliefs of the mind are the force of the soul and the moving incentives of the will. Whatever determines us to believe we call *evidence*. . . . Reason renders no account of what is evident; to condemn it to do so is to annihilate it, for it also has need of an evidence peculiar to itself. Did not reasoning rest upon principles anterior to the reason, analysis would be without end, and synthesis without commencement. The fundamental laws of belief constitute the intelligence itself; and as those laws all flow from the same source, they have the same authority; they judge by the same right; there is no appeal from the tribunal of one to that of another. Whoever revolts against any single one of these laws, revolts against them all, and so abdicates all his nature. Are there weapons of legitimate use against that faculty by which we perceive the external world? These same weapons may be turned against the conscience, the memory, the moral sense, against reason itself. . . . Let but, in any single point, the nature of knowledge—the nature, I say, and not the degree—be made subordinate to our means of knowing, and all certitude is at an end; nothing is true, nothing is false. But it is not enough to say this; for all is true and false altogether, since truth and falsehood no longer differ from sweet and bitter. The void itself is then deprived of its absolute nullity: it enters into the domain of the relative; it is something, nothing, according to the conformation of the spectator's eye. The useful is the sole subject that the understanding contemplates, the sole subject for which the heart has to make its laws. A legislation capricious and without efficacy, which applies only shifting rules to actions, and which has none for the intentions and for the desires. This is not mere declamation; all these consequences have been deduced from skeptical doctrines with an exactitude leaving nothing to be either desired or contested. It is then a fact that public and private morality, the order of society and the happiness of individuals, are directly at stake in the controversy between true philosophy and false philosophy respecting the reality of knowledge. For when existences themselves become problems, what force remains to the bond that unites them? We cannot divide the entire man; we cannot assign a part only to skepticism; as soon as skepticism once penetrates into the understanding it invades it throughout."*

I retrench nothing, change nothing in these remarkable words that express so energetically the conclusions of the common sense of mankind. I would only render them still more complete, by illustrating in its primitive and indestructible unity the fact upon which they are founded.

"We cannot divide man," says M. Royer-Collard. Here is precisely the risk that philosophical science incurs, and to which it too often succumbs. It divides man in order to study him; and after having so studied him, when it seeks to deduce from its laborious operation what man in his complete and living reality is, we find the result a strange misapprehension, because science has neglected to re-establish the unity which it broke. It puts together, it is true, the scattered members, but the being itself

*Fragments de M. Royer-Collard, in the works of Reid, translation of M. Jouffroy, vol. iv, pp. 426–451.

has disappeared; and then it is that philosophers know not how to solve the problems or to extricate themselves from the doubts by which they are confronted. Entire, living, one, the human being explained himself; mutilated and severed into distinct parts, that being loses all power and falls into obscurity.

What is sensation, what perception, judgment, reasoning, reason, will, consciousness? They are the human being, feeling, perceiving, judging, reasoning, willing, and observing what is passing within him. This is no troop of actors playing, each his part, in a complex drama; but a being single and alive, actor and sole spectator in the drama of his proper life.

What is this one and single being doing when he feels, perceives, judges, reasons, wills, and watches what is occurring within himself? He is taking cognizance at once of himself, and what is not himself. His own existence and the existence of that which is not himself, reveal themselves to him from the very first in those diverse facts and acts which philosophical science discriminates, and calls by the particular names of sensation, perception, judgment, reason, will, consciousness. The primitive and essential fact at the root of all, is the fact itself of the cognizance which man takes of himself, and of what is not himself. A cognizance, at first confused, and always incomplete, but at the same time direct and certain. Not by way of deduction, nor as a mere appearance, but by way of immediate intuition, and as a positive reality, does the human being become aware of his own existence and of that existence which is not his. This fact is lost sight of, or at least is not characterized exactly and as it is in itself, when it is said that man believes naturally and inevitably in his own existence, and in that of the external world. This is a very different thing from *belief:* it is *knowledge* itself of that double reality, internal and external, called by the name of Man and World. Philosophers ignore, and they change the nature of this fact, when, merely playing with verbal distinctions and reasonings, they condemn the human mind not to issue forth from itself, when they refuse to it the right to affirm as real, out of the mind and in itself, that which, in the mind and for the mind, the mind yet admits to be true.

The human being may deceive himself, and often does deceive himself in such or such a special affirmation as to external realities; it has of them only a knowledge incomplete, and liable to error; but its general and permanent affirmation as to their existence is still fully justified and legitimate; it knows them as it knows itself, by the same proof and by the same natural process. M. Royer-Collard expresses admirably this great fact when he says: "The universe does not exist because we perceive it; but we perceive it because it exists. . . . It needs not our presence; the absence of spectators would not make it languish away; it was before us, it will still be after us; its reality is independent of us: it is absolute."

Systematic skepticism is not, like Materialism and Pantheism, an hypothesis invented, although unsuccessfully invented, in order to solve the grand problem of soul and body, of finite and infinite; its error is not less considerable, although of a different character. It consists in a defective examination of the primitive fact of the human mind, and in the misapprehension of the nature and the import of that fact. This fact is by no means, as M. Jouffroy affirms, "a faith blind and irresistible," disavowed by rational science; it is really the natural knowledge, and the earliest knowledge acquired by the human being when it enters into activity; a knowledge, confused and incomplete, either of itself or of what is not itself; but still a knowledge direct and certain of the existence of itself, and of the existence of what is not itself. "Man believes by instinct and doubts by reason," adds M. Jouffroy; "skeptics obey the law of their instinctive nature when they believe, like the mass of mankind, in their senses, their consciousness, their memory, and when they act in consequence; so also they obey their rational nature when they confess that their beliefs are illegitimate."

This is strangely to *ignore*—I permit myself the use of this, here, incorrect expression—at once the reality of facts, and the value of words. What M. Jouffroy terms *instinct*, is the intuitive consciousness of internal reality and of external reality, and this consciousness the human being acquires directly by the complete and indivisible exercise of all his faculties; what he terms *reason* is the result of the isolated operation of one of the faculties of the human being, who virtually forgets, when he decomposes himself for his own study, what he really is. Skepticism is not the "final word of the reason respecting the reason;" it is the suicide of the reason by a negation falsely termed scientific, of natural evidence, and of the common sense of mankind.

EIGHTH MEDITATION.

IMPIETY, RECKLESSNESS, AND PERPLEXITY.

THE different systems, of each of which I have endeavored to show the essential and characteristic vice, do not remain confined to learned regions, or to the classes to which, from profession or from taste, man and the world are a special object of study. The breath of science penetrates to a distance, and pervades, unseen itself, places even where ignorance reigns. How often in remote cities and even rural districts, among a population alien to every kind of study, have I met with and discovered the traces of Rationalism, of Positivism, of Pantheism, Materialism, Skepticism; and yet these had been imported, imperceptibly and in manner that the sense could not detect, like a noxious miasma, into places where their very names were unknown; and yet they bore everywhere their natural fruits! There is a contagion in the intellectual as well as in the moral order; and the facility, the rapidity, the universality of communication, which contribute so much to the force and the grandeur of modern civilization, are as much at the disposal of evil as of good, of error as of truth.

The effects of this intellectual contagion vary with the social regions into which it penetrates, and the dispositions that it there encounters. When the systems of philosophy present themselves confusedly to minds in which ambitious and passionate feelings are fermenting, and these feelings are capable of being aided by those systems, their action is prompt and forcible. At epochs and among classes where pride and ambition of intellect reign without bounds, Rationalism and Pantheism are received with favor. In those, on the other hand, conspicuous for the almost exclusive study of the material world, or for the ardor with which men thirst after physical enjoyments, Positivism and Materialism seem very readily to prevail. After long perturbations of society, and in the midst of the disappointments and the jaded feelings that they leave behind them, many minds fall involuntarily into skepticism, or make it even their refuge. These different social facts, and the influence which they give to the different systems of philosophy, manifest themselves in our days in the state of men's minds, and they do so whether men be learned or unlearned, demonstrative or taciturn.

Three dispositions of the mind are very observable and very general—impiety, recklessness as to religion, and religious perplexity.

I feel no difficulty in thus ranging side by side things which are coexisting, and developing themselves simultaneously although contrary in their nature. There are epochs when a great current rises and hurries society toward a single object and by a single way. Others there are where different currents cross and combat one another, and impel society at the same moment toward different objects. The spirit of authority and of faith was very predominant in the seventeenth century; the spirit of independence and of innovation in the eighteenth. The nineteenth century is sweeping on its way under the empire of tendencies various but simultaneous in their power and their activity; the different principles and elements of our society, good or the reverse, confront one another, awaiting the moment when they may again be harmonized. I retraced the awakening of Christianity and its progress; I seek in no respect to qualify any remark that I have made, either as to that important movement or as to the confidence with which it inspires me; but I, at the same time, believe also in the forcible influence of the antichristian demonstrations which are taking the form of impiety or of recklessness; nor can I disregard the force of that religious perplexity into which this great struggle throws so many men of feeble purpose, and even some men of eminent powers of mind.

In our days impiety is spreading, and assuming serious development, more especially among the operative classes, and in that young generation that issues from the middle classes, and is destined to follow the liberal professions. Not that the infection is universal even there; on the contrary, those classes show also the most different tendencies; among them, too, the progress of the Christian awakening has made itself felt, and religious belief is treated with more respect. There, however, it is that the evil of impiety has its focus and its center of expansion. Sometimes it manifests itself under gross and cynical forms, sometimes with a pretension to thought and learning; now by the brutal licentiousness of its behavior, now by the arrogant yet embarrassed expression of its opinions. Last year I received an invitation to attend the great congress of students assembled at Liège; an invitation which, although I expressed for the purpose of this assemblage a real and a sincere interest, I declined. When I learned what the ideas were that had been there loudly expressed—when I read that the question had there been put as one between God and man, and that the idolatry of man had been proclaimed in the place of the adoration of God, —I experienced two sentiments the most contradictory, a lively satisfaction that I had held myself aloof from such a scene, and a profound regret, at the same time, that I had not been present to protest against such an invasion of Pantheism and of Atheism into young souls, upon whom my thoughts only rest with sentiments of affectionate hopefulness. I have grown old, I have had to undergo painful disappointments, but in spite of all, my first impulse has ever been to believe in the prompt efficacy of truth when it knocks unhesitatingly at the door of the mind; nor is it without reluctance that I bring myself to wait for time and experience to unvail what is error. Of the two kinds of impiety which I have just alluded to, the impiety which is gross and cynical, which springs from immorality and which produces immorality, is undoubtedly the more fatal to the human soul, to its dignity and its future lot; but systematic impiety—impiety that establishes itself into doctrine—is the more dangerous for human societies; for, enamored of itself, it takes its pride in self-glorification and self-propagation. The ambitious ones of impiety obtain more credit than those, the chief characteristic of whose impiety is licentiousness.

Recklessness in religion is in our days a more widely spread evil than impiety. I do not here speak of that indifferentism with respect to religious subjects that the Abbé de la Mennais so eloquently attacked; that sentiment may be profound, and it may be frivolous; it may spring from Materialism, from Skepticism, from a thoughtful impiety, as well as from a gross forgetfulness of the paramount questions which exercise the human mind. The recklessness now so common gives no thought at all to these subjects, does not picture to itself that there is any ground for so doing; where this tendency prevails, man's thought confines itself to its terrestrial, its actual life; the business and the interests of this life alone occupy him, alone content him; there is, as it were, a sleep of all those instincts and requirements of the human soul which go beyond this low region, and if not a complete abdication, at least a sluggish torpor of the heavenly part of our nature.

Let not the friends of a religious life and of the Christian faith deceive themselves; it is here that they have the greatest obstacles to encounter, the deadest weight to lift and to remove. Aggression provokes resistance; a struggle leads to the marshaling of the different hostile forces; nor does the learning of the believer dread to enter the arena with the learning of the incredulous. But recklessness in religion is like a vast Dead Sea in which no being lives, an immense barren desert in which no vegetation pushes. It is, if not the most revolting, at least the most formidable evil of the day. It is against this evil that Christians are bound, more especially, to direct their energies, for there are a world and an entire population here to be conquered.

Nor will *points d'appui* or means of action fail them in this great work. For if religious recklessness is in our days deplorably common, neither is perplexity as to religious matters a stranger among us. It springs from sentiments and out of interests very different in their natures, sometimes merely on the surface, sometimes in the depths of the soul. There is a kind of perplexity founded upon the dictates of common sense, and entitled to every respect, but to which I do not accord, nevertheless, the epithet of religious; this perplexity is generated by the instinct or the experience of the utility of religion for the maintenance of order in society, not merely in the great public society, but also in the smaller domestic societies, that is, in the state as well as in families. A man of distinguished mental capacity and of an honorable character, "elève" of the "Ecole politechnique," and "ingénieur en chef" in one of our great departments, was one day speaking to me with sorrow of the attacks leveled at Christianity. "It is not," he said, "on my own account that I regret these attacks; you know I am a 'Voltairean;' but I ask for regularity and peace in my own household; I felicitate myself that my wife is a Christian, and I mean my daughters to be brought up like Christian women. These demolishers know not what they are doing; it is not merely upon our Churches, it is upon our houses, our homes and their inmates, that their blows are telling!"

There is a perplexity more serious and more profound—a perplexity really religious—one suggested not merely by the necessity of social order, but by that of moral security, of harmony, of confidence, and of intimate hopefulness in the presence of the problems and of the chances that weigh upon man. This perplexity takes place not merely in the minds of thinking men—of men who render to themselves an account of their internal troubles, and who avow them undisguisedly; it causes agitation and spreads desolation among multitudes of single-minded, modest, and silent men, who suffer from the antichristian *malaria* spread around them. What framer of statistics shall count their number? what philosopher minister successfully to their disease?

I go further still. I listen to contemporary philosophers themselves, and I find in the cases of some of the more eminent an intellectual perplexity, showing itself clearly through opinions the most systematic, and the furthest removed from the Christian religion. I shall name but two—M. Vacherot and M. Edmond Scherer. I have no intention of entering here into a special examination of their ideas; I seek only to show the state of their minds and of their souls, as it results from the tenor of their works.

I have read, and read over again, with scrupulous attention, the two principal philosophical treatises of M. Vacherot, *La Métaphysique et la Science ou Principes de Philosophie Positive*,* and the *Essais de Philosophie Critiqué*.† M. Vacherot does not desire to be, nor is he really, in his conscience and in his own eyes, an advocate either of Materialism, or Positivism, or Pantheism, or Atheism, or Skepticism. He analyzes and he refutes successively these different systems, as conceived and expounded by their most distinguished representatives; he defends himself, and with warmth, from the charge of adhering to them: "a man," he says, "is not an Atheist, a Materialist, a Pantheist, an Idealist, because he does not believe in God, soul, mind, matter, world—in all these meta-

* Second edition, three vols. 12mo., 1863.
† One vol. 8vo., 1864.

physical words taken in a given acceptation. The true *Atheist*, if such a one exists, is he whose mind is grossly empirical, and wanting in the sense of what is intelligible, ideal, and divine. The true *Pantheist* is he who identifies truth and reality, God and the world, whether, like Spinoza and Goethe, he deifies the world, or like the Stoics, he materializes God. The true *Materialist* is he who degrades man to the beast, either by denying him his superior and really human faculties, or by deriving these from animal faculties. The true *Idealist*, like Berkeley, is he who rejects all external reality as an illusion, whatever the conception of that reality; whether it be as a thing made up of forces and of laws, or as consisting of extended matter. . . . All these words require to be defined and explained, or they necessarily occasion mysteries, contradictions, and absurdities. In their vague complexities they do not express ideas of sufficient simplicity, nor do they answer to ideas sufficiently precise for science to adopt them unreservedly and without distinction. . . . A chosen few exist whose sympathy is dear to me; I remain profoundly attached to all the truths which they, with reason, regard as constituting the strength, life, and honor of philosophy. I remain, like them, a Spiritualist, an Idealist, a Theist, although with other methods, another language, and also, beyond a doubt, with notable reservations." *

Nor is M. Vacherot more of a Skeptic than of a Materialist and a Pantheist; he believes firmly in absolute truth, in scientific metaphysics, and in the universal and essential principles which form their bases. "Metaphysics," he says, "have nothing to dread from analysis; it is a test from which they can only issue with honor. The truths *à priori* upon which the science rests, will inspire no more doubt so soon as it comes to be well understood that those truths are founded upon the ordinary prin-

* La Métaphysique et la science; in the Introduction and the Preface, vol. i., pp. xvi, xxxiv.

ciples of demonstration, like all the truths *à priori* of the other sciences. Metaphysics have, and will ever have for their object, the Being infinite, necessary, absolute, and universal. Now the ideas of being, infinite, necessary, absolute, universal, are so involved in the notion of appearance, finite, contingent, relative, individual, that it is impossible for the human mind to separate them. Accordingly, in order to be entitled to deny Metaphysics, and the truths which are peculiar to them, we must first mutilate the human mind, and reduce it to the pure faculties of sensation and imagination which are common to it with animals. From the moment when the reason, the thought, the faculty peculiar to the human intelligence, enters the field, it brings necessarily with it the object of sensation and of imagination, under the categories of quantity, quality, being, relation, unity. Then it is that appear to the mind the distinction, and afterward the logical connection, of the two terms corresponding to each category, of the finite and the infinite, of the contingent and the necessary, of the individual and the universal, of the relative and the absolute, of appearance and being. The thought enters then perforce, whether it is conscious of it or not, upon the peculiar ground of Metaphysics. Nothing but a gross and, so to say, an animal empiricism, has the right to deny the conceptions and the truths of this science, and the denial is a denegation of the higher faculties of the intelligence."*

It is impossible to disavow more indignantly Materialism, Atheism, Skepticism, with their principles and their consequences. But after all these declarations and these disavowals, when M. Vacherot has to draw his conclusions, and has to set the affirmation of his own ideas by the side of his criticism of the ideas of other writers; when he, in his turn, undertakes to explain God and the world, this twofold object of Metaphysics, the perplexity of the thinker

* La Métaphysique et la science; Preface, vol. i, p. xlviii.

becomes at once apparent, and he falls, in spite of himself, into the very paths from which he proposed to escape.

"What do you understand by God?" says he; "the perfect Being? He is the God of Plato, Aristotle, Descartes, Malebranche, Leibnitz; he is the God of all the theologians with whom *Divinity* and *Perfection* are synonyms. That God is our God too. But if, of this God, immutable in his perfection, elevated beyond time, space, the movement of universal life, you make anything else than an ideal of the thought, I confess I no longer comprehend him. . . . These ideas, all equally reducible to the idea of the *Perfect*, as understood by Plato, Descartes, Malebranche, Fénélon, Leibnitz, can have no *objective reality*, and only exist in the ideal order of pure thought; absolutely in the same manner as the figures of geometry do, which lose all the vigorousness and all the exactitude of their definition elsewhere than in the domain of the understanding. . . . Perfection exists, can only exist, in the thought. It is of the essence of perfection to be purely ideal; and the remark applies as truly to the Perfect Being of Descartes and of Leibnitz as to the 'intelligible world' of Plato and of Malebranche. A 'perfect God,' or a 'real God?' Theology must make its choice. A perfect God is only an ideal God."*

That is to say, that for Metaphysics to admit God, the *Being* God must vanish, and remain only a conception, a notion, an idea. It may be that to a philosopher or two this may seem still Theism; to the human soul, and to the human race, it is Atheism, and nothing else.

God thus made to vanish, what becomes in its turn of the world?

Here God reappears. "As for the *real* God," says M. Vacherot, "he lives, he develops himself in the immensity of space and in the eternity of time; he appears to us under the infinite

* La Métaphysique et la science; vol. i, pp. xii, 1, vol. iii, p. 247.

variety of forms which are his manifestations—he is *Cosmos*. . . . The world *thought of* is something else than the world *imagined*. Imagination represents to us the world as an immense mass of dispersed matter, as an infinite collection of forces disseminated in the vast fields of space. The idea does not occur to men of vulgar minds, nor even to our men of learning, that this image of universal life cannot for an instant support the glance of reason; they do not perceive that *void* is synonymous with *nothing*, that the atom is an unintelligible hypothesis; that *being* is always and everywhere, without any possible solution of continuity, either in time or in space; that the universal life is one in its apparent dispersion; and finally, that the world is a *being*, and not merely a *whole*." *

What is this if it be not Pantheism?

And these incoherences, these contradictions, these relapses of M. Vacherot into systems that he disavows, and that he has just combated,

La Métaphysique et la science, vol. iii, p. 247; vol. i, p. lii.

what are they but striking evidences of the vanity of his efforts, like those of so many others, to explain, unaided by God, God and the universe?

Of another nature is the perplexity of M. Edmond Scherer; his is the disquietude of the critic, not the embarrassment of the metaphysician. M. Edmond Scherer was a believing Christian, a believer zealous in his faith, and active in its cause. The examination of systems and of facts, historical criticism and philosophical criticism, impelled him to skepticism; not to that skepticism which is indifferent and strange to all personal conviction. M. Scherer believes in truth and in the rights of truth; but where that truth? He seeks it, he finds it not; he wanders among systems and facts as in a labyrinth, discovering at each step that his path is the wrong one, and from it nevertheless finding no issue. He is still aware that humanity cannot live in a labyrinth, that it requires—nay, absolutely requires—to issue forth, to behold, or at least to catch glimpses of, the light of day. He has a sentiment of the moral requirements of human nature, of man's life; and he sees well that the negations and the doubts of the different systems of philosophy can never satisfy those requirements. I have already cited, in the course of these *Meditations*, some of the passages in which this perplexity strikingly manifests itself; a perplexity full at once of pride and sadness, which, although it does not shake M. Scherer in his convictions, makes him nevertheless see their vanity.* He knows that its own thought suffices not for the human soul; perhaps it is his own soul suggests to him that knowledge.

Why is it that Christianity, in spite of all the attacks which it has had to undergo, and all the ordeals through which it has been made to pass, has for eighteen centuries satisfied

* See particularly the passage cited in the Third Meditation (Rationalism) of thisvolume, p. 256, etc., and in the "Meditation on the Essence of the Christian Religion," (Third Meditation, the Supernatural,) p. 119.

infinitely better the spontaneous instincts and invincible cravings of humanity? Is it not because it is pure from the errors which vitiate the different systems of philosophy just passed in review? because it fills up the void that those systems either create or leave in the human soul? because, in short, it conducts man higher to the fountain of light? Question paramount, to which these *Meditations* are intended as the prelude, and which I shall essay to solve, by confronting, as I before said,* Christianity with its opponents, and by showing that, if it succeeds where they fail, the reason is, that, sprung from a higher source than man, it alone has the right to succeed, for it alone knows man rightly as he is—as one entire being; it alone satisfies man by furnishing him with a rule for his guidance through life.

* First Meditation, p. 200.

THE END.

www.ingramcontent.com/pod-product-compliance
Lightning Source LLC
LaVergne TN
LVHW020120110826
845151LV00001B/223

9781425542061